The Resistance to Theory

The Resistance
to Theory

Paul de Man

Foreword by Wlad Godzich

Theory and History of Literature, Volume 33

University of Minnesota Press, Minneapolis

Published by the University of Minnesota Press
2037 University Avenue Southeast, Minneapolis MN 55414.
Published simultaneously in Canada
by Fitzhenry & Whiteside Limited, Markham.
Printed in the United States of America.
Second printing, 1987
Library of Congress Cataloging-in-Publication Data

De Man, Paul.
 The resistance to theory.

 (Theory and history of literature ; v. 33)
 Bibliography: p.
 Includes index.
 1. Criticism — Addresses, essays, lectures.
2. Literature — Philosophy — Addresses, essays, lectures.
I. Title.   II. Series.
PN85.D374 1986   801'.95   85-28820
ISBN 0-8166-1293-5
ISBN 0-8166-1294-3 (pbk.)

The following works are reproduced with permission of the originating publisher: "The Resistance to Theory," *Yale French Studies* 63 (1982); "The Return to Philology," *Times Literary Supplement*, Dec. 10, 1982; "Hypogram and Inscription," *Diacritics* 11 (1981), the Johns Hopkins University Press; "Dialogue and Dialogism," *Poetics Today* 4:1 (1983) the Porter Institute for Poetics and Semiotics, Tel Aviv University; "Bibliography of Texts by Paul de Man," *Yale French Studies* 69 (1985.)

"An interview with Paul de Man," commissioned by RAI (The Italian National Broadcasting System), broadcast June 1, 1983, is reprinted with permission of the author © 1983 from Maurizio Ferraris and Stefano Rosso (eds.), *Decostruzione tra filosofia e letteratura*, special issue of *Nuova Corrente*, vol. XXXI (1984) n. 93-94, pp. 303-13.

"Reading and History" first appeared as the introduction to Hans Robert Jauss's *Toward an Aesthetic of Reception* (Minneapolis: University of Minnesota Press, 1982). "Conclusions: Walter Benjamin's 'Task of the Translator'" was given as the last in a series of six Messenger Lectures at Cornell University on March 4, 1983; the question-and-answer session followed the lecture.

Contents

Theory and History of Literature
Edited by Wlad Godzich and Jochen Schulte-Sasse

Foreword
The Tiger on the Paper Mat
Wlad Godzich

I

After the publication of *Allegories of Reading* in 1979, Paul de Man found himself constantly besieged by requests for articles, introductions, conference papers, and other forms of scholarly communication. Whereas some scholars live in a tragic mode, the disjunction between what they consider their proper intellectual pursuits and the demands made upon them by their profession, Paul de Man had come to think of this disjunction as the relation between the contingency of the historical and the necessity of coherent thought, with the former imposing a salutary heterogeneity upon the latter's inevitable drift toward single-minded totalization. Though he remained steadfast in his concerns, as anyone who has read his work from the earliest essays to the very last ones will readily acknowledge, he framed them according to the demands of the moment in which they were ultimately written, and he drew a certain pleasure from the ironies that attended their publication.

The very number of calls made upon de Man in these years and his ability to write a great many major pieces in rapid succession eventually led him, in late 1981 and early 1982, to formulate a general plan for publishing in book form the essays that he had been writing and that he planned to write in the near future. The present book was conceived as a unit of this general plan.

While he was properly suspicious of most forms of articulation, and particularly of those that claimed the ability to periodize, de Man did not fail to recognize their heuristic value, especially when it came to such mundane matters as publication. During the discussions that led to the formulation of the plan of publication, he put forward the following organization of his writings. His first essays (soon to be available in this series) constitute the properly *critical* face of his activity. In them he considered authors as classical as Montaigne and as modern as Borges and wondered about the present possibilities of poetry or of the historical sense in America. The very practice of such criticism led him to question its validity, an interrogation soon exacerbated by the fact that he had entered the academic profession at a time when the New Criticism was extending its hegemony over the teaching of literature in American universities. He thus began to concern himself more with matters of methodology and to write about the works of other critics rather than those of poets or novelists. The results of this phase of his work are to be found in the revised edition of *Blindness and Insight*. It is in the essays gathered in that volume that Paul de Man articulated a stance that was properly *theoretical*, and while he was not alone to do so then, his adoption of such a stance proved to be very influential in American academic circles.

He did not entirely welcome this influence for a number of reasons, not the least of which had to do with his own misgivings with respect to the theoretical instance so enthusiastically embraced in some quarters and denounced with equal eagerness and passion in others. In the course of these theoretical essays de Man had come to delimit a problematic that was fundamental to him, but which until then had been mediated through categories of consciousness and temporality inherited from the Hegelian substratum of phenomenology: *the matter of reading*. Reading, as de Man began to conceive of it, is far more radical than any theoretical enterprise can admit. As we shall see later, reading disrupts the continuity between the theoretical and the phenomenal and thus forces a recognition of the incompatibility of language and intuition. Since the latter constitutes the foundational basis of cognition upon which perception, consciousness, experience, and the logic and the understanding, not to mention the aesthetics that are attendant to them, are constructed, there results a wholesale shakeout in the organization and conceptualization of knowledge, from which language, conceived as a double system of tropes and persuasion, that is as a rhetorical entity, emerges as the unavoidable dimensionality of all cognition. This was the view first adumbrated in ''The Rhetoric of Temporality'' and developed in *Allegories of Reading*. There followed a number of essays, now collected in *The Rhetoric of Romanticism*, in which implications of this conception of reading were explored over a historically circumscribed corpus.

De Man realized that the conception of reading that he had uncovered in his own theoretical essays had to overcome two major obstacles: the first is posed by the theoretical enterprise itself, while the second has to do with the history of philosophical thought since the eighteenth century. He thus formulated two projects to deal with these problems, neither of which was finished at the time of his death in December 1983, though both were very far advanced toward completion. The second, to be published shortly in this series, came to be entitled *The Aesthetic Ideology*, and it contains essays that focus on how the radical nature of Kant's conception of aesthetic judgment — which approximates de Man's own notion of the radicalness of reading — was given a more reassuring path in Schiller's interpretation and in its subsequent fate in the philosophical tradition. Aesthetic judgment came to be replaced or overlaid by an ideological construct of values, now commonly taken to be the aesthetic, even though, de Man insists, the underlying judgment will not support such an overlay but will actively work to dismantle it. Only an activity such as reading can come in touch with this process and experience the resistance of the material to the ideological overlay. The shape of the volume is apparent, though Paul de Man did not live to write two essays that would have been of considerable interest: one on Kierkegaard as seen by Adorno, and the other on Marx's *The German Ideology*. This collection of essays thus represents, among other things, de Man's intervention in the current debates on modernity and postmodernity.

The essays gathered in the present volume were meant to reexamine the work of other theorists, in a manner somewhat analogous to that found in *Blindness and Insight*, in order to determine what about the theoretical enterprise itself blinds it to the radicalness of reading and in order to disengage the principle of this blindness, which de Man came to conceive of as a "resistance" for reasons I shall attempt to explore later. This volume too is unfinished. From the outset it was meant to include three essays of which two appear here in preparatory form and one not at all: essays on Bakhtin and on Benjamin, for which the papers included here were early versions still to be revised, and an essay on Kenneth Burke, which Paul de Man wanted very much to write for quite some time and which he considered the "social" counterpart to the more "formalist" essay on Riffaterre included here, though equally meant to arrive at a notion of inscription that would wreak havoc with the attempt to deal with history and the social only through its representational forms.

This brief outline gives a sense of the direction that Paul de Man felt his work was taking when he was struck down by illness. He labored hard to bring it to completion, taking advantage of every moment of remission, though quite aware that the task he had embarked upon would always remain incomplete. The texts he has left behind invite us to pursue his reflexion, challenging us to read them in the radical way he had begun to formulate.

Again, the account I give here is not meant to be canonical nor does it represent more than a punctual attempt to rationalize the publication in book form of essays written for the bewildering array of occasions that mobilize present-day scholarship. From a more thematic perspective, one could formulate different articulations of the de Man oeuvre, with pivotal roles going to essays such as "Heidegger's Exegeses of Hölderlin," "The Rhetoric of Temporality," and "Shelley

Disfigured." But the articulation that I describe governs the publication of Paul de Man's essays and, as such, it is likely to play a role in the mode of their reading, even if it is to be no more but no less than a certain form of resistance.

II

All the essays in this volume engage the question of theory as it has come to dominate our literary scene, and since theory is primarily a concern of academically situated scholars, the essays also touch upon questions of pedagogy and institutional determination, although de Man did not feel that the latter was as important in the North American context as in the European one (cf. his interview in this volume, which was broadcast in part on the cultural service of RAI International, in which he usefully distinguishes between his attitude and that of Derrida in this respect). The title of the volume is borrowed from one of the essays which originally bore quite a different title, but whose retitling brings together all the questions of theory, pedagogy, and institutionalization that are among the principal themes of this volume, along with the figure of resistance which is attached to them here.

The essay "The Resistance to Theory" was originally entitled "Literary Theory: Aims and Methods." It was commissioned by the Committee on Research Activities of the Modern Language Association for its volume *Introduction to Scholarship in Modern Languages and Literatures* where it was to figure as the section on literary theory. Paul de Man found it difficult to write the pedagogical piece that was expected of him and wrote instead an essay in which he attempted to determine the nature of the resistance that theory poses to its own definition. The essay he submitted encountered a resistance of another kind: it was judged inappropriate for the volume the MLA was producing and an altogether different essay was then commissioned from Paul Hernadi. De Man did not quarrel with this judgment; he simply retitled the essay for oral delivery at Amherst College in the spring of 1981 and determined soon thereafter that it should provide the title of the collection on theory that he was then contemplating.

The sequence of events in this little brouhaha ought to make clear that the term "resistance" refers only secondarily, and almost ironically, to the institutional forms of resistance to theory as they were experienced in the seventies and eighties in the United States. Although de Man did anticipate some form of such resistance to his essay, as the introductory paragraphs make clear, he used the term in the essay itself with a very different view in mind. As is almost always the case with his coinages, the figures he puts into motion in his texts have a technical meaning which it is useful to recall.

The term resistance names a property of matter recognized since antiquity: its perceptibility to touch and inertial opposition to muscular exertion. For Aristotle, *ta physika* are characterized by the resistance they oppose to us and they thus become objects of our cognition: it is by virtue of this resistance that we know them to be outside of ourselves and not illusions fostered upon us by our unreliable sensory apparatus. Resistance is a property of the referent, we would say today, which allows this referent to become the object of knowledge of the subject that we are. Without this resistance, we would never be able to ascertain whether the phenomenal or the sensible is really "out there" and thus whether we have any knowledge of such an "out there." To the extent that theory has cognitive pretensions, resistance is very important to it as a precondition for the theory's cognitive reach into the phenomenal. This is a venerable problem not only of literary theory but of language philosophy, as the following passage in the essay seems to indicate in its recondite way:

> If a cat is called a tiger it can easily be dismissed as a paper tiger; the question remains however why one was so scared of the cat in the first place. The same tactic works in reverse: calling the cat a mouse and then deriding it for its pretense to be mighty. Rather than being drawn into this polemical whirlpool, it might be better to try to call the cat a cat and to document, however briefly, the contemporary version of the resistance to theory in this country. (infra, p. 5)

Passages such as this one are not at all rare in de Man's writings. One may think for example, of the justly famous play on Archie Bunker/archè debunker in "Semiology and Rhetoric." As in that passage, we seem to have an instance of postmodern writing here with its borrowings of current political slogans ("paper tiger"), popular culture (Mighty Mouse of Saturday morning television cartoon fare), paronomasia ("deriding"), etc. And its cognitive dimension is to be found in what Riffaterre would call the conversion of a matrix: instead of "to call a spade a spade" we have "to call a cat a cat," an apparent reaffirmation of the feline code of the passage, but since the meaning of "to call a spade a spade" is that of the primacy of denomination over decorum, or in somewhat different terms, of denotation over connotation, we have a version of a famous conundrum of language philosophy and of the philosophy of mind: "the cat is on the mat." In other words, the problem is that of the cognitive dimension of language: how it apprehends the real. And in the play on the size of the cat and on its putative fearsomeness, de Man further alludes to his own discussion, and to Derrida's, of the famous passage on the "giant" in Rousseau in which the relation of figural language to denotation is explored. All of which are certified theoretical problems, indeed topoi of recent theory.

It may be useful at this juncture to recall what theory is. Presently we tend to use the term to mean a system of concepts that aims to give a global explanation to an area of knowledge, and we oppose it to praxis by virtue of the fact that it is a form of speculative knowledge. The term obviously has taken on this meaning after Kant, though it appears in most of the western languages earlier, by way of Latin translations from the Greek (with a rather interesting swerve through Arabic that we need not concern ourselves with here). Etymologically, the term comes from the Greek verb *theorein*, to look at, to contemplate, to survey. And in Greek, it does not enter into an opposition with praxis — an opposition constructed in Idealist philosophy and eventually used to combat the latter — but rather with *aesthesis*, something that Ruskin recalls in his *Modern Painters*:

> The impressions of beauty . . . are neither sensual nor intellectual but moral, and for the faculty receiving them . . . no term can be more accurate . . . than that employed by the Greeks, "theoretic" which I pray permission to use and to call the operation of the faculty itself "Theoria." (II, iii, par. 1, and then again in paragraph 8:) The mere animal consciousness of the pleasantness I call Aesthesis, but the exulting, reverent, and grateful perception of it I call Theoria.

Ruskin articulates the opposition between *aesthesis* and *theoria* around the matter-of-factness of the first and the jubilatory character of the second without inquiring into the provenance of this jubilation.

The latter is indeed well attested. It comes from the fact that the act of looking at, of surveying, designated by *theorein* does not designate a private act carried out by a cogitating philosopher but a very public one with important social consequences. The Greeks designated certain individuals, chosen on the basis of their probity and their general standing in the polity, to act as legates on certain formal occasions in other city states or in matters of considerable political importance. These individuals bore the title of *theoros*, and collectively constituted a *theoria*. (It may be useful to bear in mind that the word is always a plural collective.) They were summoned on special occasions to attest the occurrence of some event, to witness its happenstance, and to then verbally certify its having taken place. (We may recall here the role of witnesses to the execution of death sentences in the American judicial system.) In other words, their function was one of see-and-tell. To be sure, other individuals in the city could see and tell, but their telling was no more than a *claim* that they had seen something, and it needed some authority to adjudicate the validity of such a claim. The city needed a more official and more ascertainable form of knowledge if it was not to lose itself in endless claims and counterclaims. The *theoria* provided such a bedrock of certainty: what it certified as having seen could become the object of public discourse. The individual citizen, indeed even women, slaves, and children, were capable of aesthesis, that is perception, but these perceptions had no social standing. They were not sanctioned and thus could not form the basis of deliberation, judgment, and action in the polity. Only the theoretically attested event could be treated as a fact. The institutional nature of this certification ought not to escape us, as well as its social inscription. Indeed, it may be of more than theoretical interest, in our current sense of the term, to wonder how this social dimension of the certification of events, of the granting to something the discursive standing of "real," came to be occulted, though that would take us too far afield from our immediate concerns.

The structure of the functioning of the Greek *theoria* is as follows then: between the event and its entry into public discourse, there is a mediating instance invested with undeniable authority by the polity. This authority effects the passage from the seen to the told, it puts into socially acceptable and reliable language what it apprehends. This authority, the *theoria*, has to use language itself though, and its language is not yet covered by the guarantees it brings to the polity. In fact, it must construct that guarantee within itself, although the *theoria* is alone socially recognized as capable of wielding such language. The structure of such a language must be of a nature to permit the following, admittedly awkward paraphrase: "We who now address you here, were there then and we witnessed there then what we are about to tell you here now in order that you here and we here may all talk here now and in the future about how what happened there then affects us here." In other words, such a language must be deictically articulated, something that did not escape Hegel as he embarked on his own theoretical project in *The Phenomenology of Mind* with a consideration of the "this." And it is the problematic in the background of "the cat is on the mat" discussion, the famous paper tiger of the philosophy of language and mind. One understands more readily why jubilation attended to the theoretical among the Greeks: they had solved the problem until philosophers came along and attempted to ground everything in sense perception, in aesthesis, with a theorizing of their own, appropriated from the *polis* in ways as yet little understood, as the sole mediation.

III

Deixis is the linguistic mechanism that permits the articulation of all of these distinctions between the here and the there, the now and the then, the we and the you. It establishes the existence of an "out there" that is not an "over here," and thus it is fundamental to the theoretical enterprise. It gives it its authority. "The cat is on the mat" problem is a problem of deixis: the sentence is true only insofar as the utterer refers to a given cat, that is the cat is a cat that has been referred to or otherwise brought to the attention of the addressee. For all practical purposes, the sentence must be taken to mean something like: "this cat that you and I are aware of is now on this mat that you and I are aware of." Of course none of us speaks in this way, just as the *theoria* did not speak in the way that I indicated earlier, but the proper functioning of the discourse that we wield presupposes that sort of structural capacity to specify deixis. The history of languages is instructive in this regard: it is well known that the present-day articles of Romance languages are descendants of Latin demonstratives, and the medieval forms of these articles still had strong demonstrative capabilities and have to be translated as such. Many utterances can be evaluated in terms of their claims to truthfulness only when this deictic dimension is brought into consideration. Neither the logical nor the grammatical structure of a sentence suffices for these purposes; they may only provide assurances of well-formedness but they are helpless to determine whether the sentence is true with respect to a certain state of affairs.

Theories of language have been aware of this problem for a long time, and it is indeed the Stoics who came to give this problem the name of deixis. Modern linguistics has refined it, and the present canonical form of the problem is one articulated in rapid succession by Emile Benveniste and Roman Jakobson, who made explicit the role played by the act of uttering in the functioning of deixis. Benveniste in his "Formal Apparatus of Enunciation" (*Problèmes de linguistique générale,* Paris, 1966) identifies the specificity of the deictics with the fact that they refer to the instance of discourse: they have no objective referents outside of the discourse; they actually make reference to what has no referent since their meaning is determinable only by means of the instance of discourse that they occur in. Benveniste then activates the Saussurean opposition of *langue* and *parole* to conclude that deictics are the verbal mechanism that permits language to become discourse, that is they effect the passage from the virtuality of *langue* to the actuality of *parole*. Jakobson's analysis of deictics, which he calls "shifters," is quite similar though it originates in, and indeed closely espouses, Peircian notions on the subject.

What is interesting about this theory of deixis is that it appears to run counter to what seemed to be the very core of the problem. On the one hand, the indicational capability of deixis, its ability to indicate a here and now, had been taken as the very bedrock of referentiality. This is where language encountered the *resistance* of what it talked about, and thus it had cognitive value; it apprehended the world. On the other hand, once the mechanism at work in deixis was investigated and described, it turns out that deictics do not refer to anything tangible, to anything that has any resistance, as is clear from the very instability of the terms themselves (I becomes you when you address me, and here turns into there, etc.). Deictics refer to the instance of discourse, Benveniste tells us, and this is a dismal finding for those who placed their hope in the referential capacity of language for it is clear that deictics were the great hope of referentiality. But it would be too quick to conclude that, as a result, deictics lock us into language.

Deictics do refer; they refer to the fact that language has taken place and that it is something that takes place, that is even something that offers resistance. Benveniste's reliance upon the Saussurean terminology and its Aristotelian overtones ought not to blind us to the fact that deictics are the means by which language makes itself into *something that takes place and something that can be referred to*, and it is from this inaugural act of reference that all other forms of reference will flow. It is, in the terminology that de Man uses, the resistance of language to language that grounds all other forms of resistance. To language, all of the real is fungible but itself, and the resistance that language opposes to itself — which may take the form of troping — establishes the reality of language to language, which then constructs all other forms of reference upon this fundamental model. In terms of the opposition that Heidegger has reconstructed from antiquity, the taking place of language (enunciation in Benveniste's terminology) is its ontological dimension, whereas the type of reference that takes place within the space opened up by the inaugural act of language's taking place is the ontic.

The ontic comes to deploy itself in the space that the ontological has opened up for it. This inaugural act of opening up a space de Man formulates as *inscription*, and one can readily see that the very deployment of the ontic requires the effacement of the ontological, hence a dialectic, in the Kantian and not the Hegelian sense, of inscription and effacement, which in this book on theory comes to replace the earlier dialectic of blindness and insight characteristic of criticism.

The problematics of inscription, worked out in the essay on Riffaterre in this volume, rejoins an older preoccupation of Paul de Man, namely history. It may be useful in this regard to compare briefly his itinerary with that of Hegel, against which much of this thinking takes place, an *against* that has to be taken to mean both in opposition to and in the sense of resting against.

In his *Phenomenology of Spirit*, Hegel too analyzed deixis through the act of indication as he embarked upon his examination of the relationship of sense certainty to cognition. He came to the conclusion that to show something, that is to apprehend its this-ness, necessitates a recognition of the fact that sense certainty is a dialectical process of negation and mediation. This process affects natural consciousness — Hegel's operative notion in this text — which puts itself forward as the unmediated and the immediate, but is shown in the analysis of showing not to be a given but a *Geschichte*, that is a history. This type of history belongs to the ontic, since it is the result of mediation and is in the realm of representation. Paul de Man came early to understand that this articulation of history depended upon the central position of consciousness, and his own early preoccupation with this category, which has led some to believe that he was somehow affiliated with the Geneva school, was an attempt to dislodge consciousness from the central position it occupied in the Hegelian edifice. When de Man came into contact with the thought of Heidegger, almost contrapuntally in the French environment in which he lived then since it was Hegel that the French were discovering then as they were finally beginning to translate him, he recognized a preoccupation similar to his own, and in the distinction of the ontic and the ontological, the possibility of distinguishing a history that is caught up in representation and one that is not. And while such a possibility was present in

Hegel's thought, it was under the sway of the dialectic which effectively robbed it of its radicality.

In Heidegger, however, the distinction between *Historie* and *Geschichte*, which maps the two different conceptions of the historical dimension, lends itself somewhat easily to certain forms of recuperation, best exemplified by the success of Heideggerian ideas in theological circles. The historical dimension that presides over the constitution of the apparent and is itself not of the apparent, to speak the language of idealist philosophy, can far too rapidly be conceived as a form of transcendentalism that effectively removes history from human view.

The problematic status of praxis in contemporary thought derives in great part from this situation. Conceived of in relation to theory, praxis is subject to the latter, and when the latter runs into problems, praxis appears arbitrary or willful. Indeed willfulness, whether constructed immediately as such or conceived along the lines of desire, has figured prominently in recent thought as a way out of this predicament. Paul de Man seems to have adopted another strategy, one that led him to recognize that the mapping of the opposition/dependency of theory and praxis, left aesthetics free standing. In a first movement, he restores the ancient relation between *aesthesis* and *theoria* and problematizes their relation, and most of us have followed with considerable interest what he has done there. But we ought not lose sight of the fact that de Man's remapping has liberated praxis from the hold that theory has had over it. It is incumbent upon us now to deal with praxis, though it becomes rapidly clear that our old ways of dealing with it, beholden as they were to the supremacy of theory and the autonomy of *aesthesis*, will not do. Praxis thus stands as a rather mysterious entity presently, the figure of the agency (*Handlung*) that we thought we had lost when we secularized but that now returns without the godhead that adorned it, as the figure of history.

The death of Paul de Man is thus a great loss as he was beginning to move into this phase of his thinking, which was going to become apparent in the essays on Burke, Kierkegaard, and Marx. But there is enough for us to *read* here, and for quite a while.

The Resistance to Theory

The Resistance to Theory

This essay was not originally intended to address the question of teaching directly, although it was supposed to have a didactic and an educational function — which it failed to achieve. It was written at the request of the Committee on Research Activities of the Modern Language Association as a contribution to a collective volume entitled *Introduction to Scholarship in Modern Languages and Literatures*. I was asked to write the section on literary theory. Such essays are expected to follow a clearly determined program: they are supposed to provide the reader with a select but comprehensive list of the main trends and publications in the field, to synthesize and classify the main problematic areas and to lay out a critical and programmatic projection of the solutions which can be expected in the foreseeable future. All this with a keen awareness that, ten years later, someone will be asked to repeat the same exercise.

I found it difficult to live up, in minimal good faith, to the requirements of this program and could only try to explain, as concisely as possible, why the main theoretical interest of literary theory consists in the impossibility of its definition. The Committee rightly judged that this was an inauspicious way to achieve the pedagogical objectives of the volume and commissioned another article. I thought their decision altogether justified, as well as interesting in its implications for the teaching of literature.

I tell this for two reasons. First, to explain the traces in the article of the original assignment which account for the awkwardness of trying to be more retrospective and more general than one can legitimately hope to be. But, second, because the predicament also reveals a question of general interest: that of the

3

relationship between the scholarship (the key word in the title of the MLA volume), the theory, and the teaching of literature.

Overfacile opinion notwithstanding, teaching is not primarily an intersubjective relationship between people but a cognitive process in which self and other are only tangentially and contiguously involved. The only teaching worthy of the name is scholarly, not personal; analogies between teaching and various aspects of show business or guidance counseling are more often than not excuses for having abdicated the task. Scholarship has, in principle, to be eminently teachable. In the case of literature, such scholarship involves at least two complementary areas: historical and philological facts as the preparatory condition for understanding, and methods of reading or interpretation. The latter is admittedly an open discipline, which can, however, hope to evolve by rational means, despite internal crises, controversies and polemics. As a controlled reflection on the formation of method, theory rightly proves to be entirely compatible with teaching, and one can think of numerous important theoreticians who are or were also prominent scholars. A question arises only if a tension develops between methods of understanding and the knowledge which those methods allow one to reach. If there is indeed something about literature, as such, which allows for a discrepancy between truth and method, between *Wahrheit* and *Methode*, then scholarship and theory are no longer necessarily compatible; as a first casualty of this complication, the notion of "literature as such" as well as the clear distinction between history and interpretation can no longer be taken for granted. For a method that cannot be made to suit the "truth" of its object can only teach delusion. Various developments, not only in the contemporary scene but in the long and complicated history of literary and linguistic instruction, reveal symptoms that suggest that such a difficulty is an inherent focus of the discourse about literature. These uncertainties are manifest in the hostility directed at theory in the name of ethical and aesthetic values, as well as in the recuperative attempts of theoreticians to reassert their own subservience to these values. The most effective of these attacks will denounce theory as an obstacle to scholarship and, consequently, to teaching. It is worth examining whether, and why, this is the case. For if this is indeed so, then it is better to fail in teaching what should not be taught than to succeed in teaching what is not true.

A general statement about literary theory should not, in theory, start from pragmatic considerations. It should address such questions as the definition of literature (what is literature?) and discuss the distinction between literary and non-literary uses of language, as well as between literary and non-verbal forms of art. It should then proceed to the descriptive taxonomy of the various aspects and species of the literary genus and to the normative rules that are bound to follow from such a classification. Or, if one rejects a scholastic for a phenomenological model, one should attempt a phenomenology of the literary activity as writing, reading or both, or of the literary work as the product, the correlate of such an activity. Whatever the approach taken (and several other theoretically justifiable starting-points can be imagined) it is certain that considerable difficulties will arise at once, difficulties that cut so deep that even the most elementary task of scholarship, the delimitation of the corpus and the *état présent* of the question, is bound to end in confusion, not necessarily because the bibliography is so large but because it is impossible to fix its borderlines. Such predictable difficulties have not prevented many writers on literature from proceeding along theoretical rather than pragmatic lines, often with considerable success. It can be shown however that, in all cases, this success depends on the power of a system (philosophical, religious or ideological) that may well remain implicit but that determines an *a priori* conception of what is "literary" by starting out from the premises of the system rather than from the literary thing itself — if such a "thing" indeed exists. This last qualification is of course a real question which in fact accounts for the predictability of the difficulties just alluded to: if the condition of existence of an entity is itself particularly critical, then the theory of this entity is bound to fall back into the pragmatic. The difficult and inconclusive history of literary theory indicates that this is indeed the case for literature in an even more manifest manner than for other verbalized occurrences such as jokes, for example, or even dreams. The attempt to treat literature theoretically may as well resign itself to the fact that it has to start out from empirical considerations.

Pragmatically speaking, then, we know that there has been, over the last fifteen to twenty years, a strong interest in something called literary theory and that, in the United States, this interest has at times coincided with the importation and reception of foreign, mostly but not always continental, influences. We also know that this wave of interest now seems to be receding as some satiation or disappointment sets in after the initial enthusiasm. Such an ebb and flow is natural enough, but it remains interesting, in this case, because it makes the depth of the resistance to literary theory so manifest. It is a recurrent strategy of any anxiety to defuse what it considers threatening by magnification or minimization, by attributing to it claims to power of which it is bound to fall short. If a cat is called a tiger it can easily be dismissed as a paper tiger; the question remains however why one was so scared of the cat in the first place. The same tactic works in reverse: calling the cat a mouse and then deriding it for its pretense to be mighty. Rather than being drawn into this polemical whirlpool, it might be better to try to call the cat a cat and to document, however briefly, the contemporary version of the resistance to theory in this country.

The predominant trends in North American literary criticism, before the nineteen sixties, were certainly not averse to theory, if by theory one understands the rooting of literary exegesis and of critical evaluation in a system of some conceptual generality. Even the most intuitive, empirical and theoretically low-key writers on literature made use of a minimal set of concepts (tone, organic form, allusion, tradition, historical situation, etc.) of at least some general import. In several other cases, the interest in theory was publicly asserted and practiced. A broadly shared methodology, more or less overtly proclaimed, links together such influential text books of the era as *Understanding Poetry* (Brooks and Warren), *Theory of Literature* (Wellek and Warren) and *The Fields of Light* (Reuben Brower) or such theoretically oriented works as *The Mirror and the Lamp*, *Language as Gesture* and *The Verbal Icon*.

Yet, with the possible exception of Kenneth Burke and, in some respects, Northrop Frye, none of these authors would have considered themselves theoreticians in the post-1960 sense of the term, nor did their work provoke as strong reactions, positive or negative, as that of later theoreticians. There were polemics, no doubt, and differences in approach that cover a wide spectrum of divergencies, yet the fundamental curriculum of literary studies as well as the talent and training expected for them were not being seriously challenged. New Critical approaches experienced no difficulty fitting into the academic establishments without their practitioners having to betray their literary sensibilities in any way; several of its represenatives pursued successful parallel careers as poets or novelists next to their academic functions. Nor did they experience difficulties with regard to a national tradition which, though certainly less tyrannical than its European counterparts, is nevertheless far from powerless. The perfect embodiment of the New Criticism remains, in many respects, the personality and the ideology of T. S. Eliot, a combination of original talent, traditional learning, verbal wit and moral earnestness, an Anglo-American blend of intellectual gentility not so repressed as not to afford tantalizing glimpses of darker psychic and political depths, but without breaking the surface of an ambivalent decorum that has its own complacencies and seductions. The normative principles of such a literary ambiance are cultural and ideological rather than theoretical, oriented towards the integrity of a social and historical self rather than towards the impersonal consistency that theory requires. Culture allows for, indeed advocates, a degree of cosmopolitanism, and the literary spirit of the American Academy of the fifties was anything but provincial. It had no difficulty appreciating and assimilating outstanding products of a kindred spirit that originated in Europe: Curtius, Auerbach, Croce, Spitzer, Alonso, Valéry and also, with the exception of some of his works, J. P. Sartre. The inclusion of Sartre in this list is important, for it indicates that the dominant cultural code we are trying to evoke cannot simply be assimilated to a political polarity of the left and the right, of the academic and non-academic, of Greenwich Village and Gambier, Ohio. Politically oriented and predominantly non-academic journals, of which the *Partisan Review* of the fifties remains the best example, did not (after due allowance is made for all proper reservations and distinctions) stand in any genuine opposition to the New Critical approaches. The broad, though negative, consensus that brings these extremely diverse trends and individuals together is their shared resistance to theory. This diagnosis is borne out by the arguments and complicities that have since come to light in a more articulate opposition to the common opponent.

The interest of these considerations would be at most anecdotal (the historical impact of twentieth-century literary discussion being so slight) if it were not for the theoretical implications of the resistance to theory. The local manifestations of this resistance are themselves systematic enough to warrant one's interest.

What is it that is being threatened by the approaches to literature that developed during the sixties and that now, under a variety of designations, make up the ill-defined and somewhat chaotic field of literary theory? These approaches cannot be simply equated with any particular method or country. Structuralism was not the only trend to dominate the stage, not even in France, and structuralism as well as semiology are inseparable from prior tendencies in the Slavic domain. In Germany, the main impulses have come from other directions, from the Frankfurt school and more orthodox Marxists, from post-Husserlian phenomenology and post-Heideggerian hermeneutics, with only minor inroads made by structural analysis. All these trends have had their share of influence in the United States, in more or less productive combinations with nationally rooted concerns. Only a nationally or personally competitive view of history would wish to hierarchize such hard-to-label movements. The possibility of doing literary theory, which is by no means to be taken for granted, has itself become a consciously reflected-upon question and those who have progressed furthest in this question are the most controversial but also the best sources of information. This certainly includes several of the names loosely connected with structuralism, broadly enough defined to include Saussure, Jakobson and Barthes as well as Greimas and Althusser, that is to say, so broadly defined as to be no longer of use as a meaningful historical term.

Literary theory can be said to come into being when the approach to literary texts is no longer based on non-linguistic, that is to say historical and aesthetic, considerations or, to put it somewhat less crudely, when the object of discussion is no longer the meaning or the value but the modalities of production and of reception of meaning and of value prior to their establishment — the implication being that this establishment is problematic enough to require an autonomous discipline of critical investigation to consider its possibility and its status. Literary history, even when considered at the furthest remove from the platitudes of positivistic historicism, is still the history of an understanding of which the possibility is taken for granted. The question of the relationship between aesthetics and meaning is more complex, since aesthetics apparently has to do with the *effect* of meaning rather than with its content *per se*. But aesthetics is in fact, ever since its development just before and with Kant, a phenomenalism of a process of meaning and understanding, and it may be naive in that it postulates (as its name indicates) a phenomenology of art and of literature which may well be what is at issue. Aesthetics is part of a universal system of philosophy rather than a specific theory. In the nineteenth-century philosophical tradition, Nietzsche's challenge of the system erected by Kant, Hegel and their successors is a version of the general question of philosophy. Nietzsche's critique of metaphysics includes, or starts out from, the aesthetic, and the same could be argued for Heidegger. The invocation of prestigious philosophical names does not intimate that the present-day development of literary theory is a by-product of larger philosophical speculations. In some rare cases, a direct link may exist between philosophy and literary theory. More frequently, however, contemporary literary theory is a relatively autonomous version of questions that also surface, in a different context, in philosophy, though not necessarily in a clearer and more rigorous form. Philosophy, in England as well as on the Continent, is less freed from traditional patterns than it sometimes pretends to believe and the prominent, though never dominant, place of aesthetics among the main components of the system is a constitutive part of this system. It is therefore not surprising that contemporary literary theory came into being from outside philosophy and sometimes in conscious rebellion against the weight of its tradition. Literary theory may now well have become a legitimate concern of philosophy but it cannot be assimilated to it, either factually or theoretically. It contains a necessarily pragmatic moment that certainly weakens it as theory but that adds a subversive element of unpredictability and makes it something of a wild card in the serious game of the theoretical disciplines.

The advent of theory, the break that is now so often being deplored and that sets it aside from literary history and from literary criticism, occurs with the introduction of linguistic terminology in the metalanguage about literature. By linguistic terminology is meant a terminology that designates reference prior to designating the referent and takes into account, in the consideration of the world, the referential function of language or, to be somewhat more specific, that considers reference as a function of language and not necessarily as an intuition. Intuition implies perception, consciousness, experience, and leads at once into the world of logic and of understanding with all its correlatives, among which aesthetics occupies a prominent place. The assumption that there can be a science of language which is not necessarily a logic leads to the development of a terminology which is not necessarily aesthetic. Contemporary literary theory comes into its own in such events as the application of Saussurian linguistics to literary texts.

The affinity between structural linguistics and literary texts is not as obvious as, with the hindsight of history, it now may seem. Peirce, Saussure, Sapir and Bloomfield were not originally concerned with literature at all but with the scientific foundations of linguistics. But the interest of philologists such as Roman Jakobson or literary critics such as Roland Barthes in semiology reveals the natural attraction of literature to a theory of linguistic signs. By considering language as a system of signs and of signification rather than as an established pattern of meanings, one displaces or even suspends the traditional barriers between literary and presumably non-literary uses of language and liberates the corpus from the secular weight of textual canonization. The results of the encounter between semiology and literature went considerably further than those of many other theoretical models — philological, psychological or classically epistemological — which writers on literature in quest of such models had tried out before. The responsiveness of literary texts to semiotic analysis is visible in that, whereas other approaches were unable to reach beyond observations that could be paraphrased or translated in terms of common knowledge, these analyses revealed patterns that could only be described in terms of their own, specifically linguistic, aspects. The linguistics of semiology and of literature apparently have something in common that only their shared perspective can detect and that pertains distinctively to them. The definition of this something, often referred to as literariness, has become the object of literary theory.

Literariness, however, is often misunderstood in a way that has provoked much of the confusion which dominates today's polemics. It is frequently assumed, for instance, that literariness is another word for, or another mode of, aesthetic response. The use, in conjunction with literariness, of such terms as style and stylistics, form or even "poetry" (as in "the poetry of grammar"), all of which carry strong aesthetic connotations, helps to foster this confusion, even among those who first put the term in circulation. Roland Barthes, for example, in an essay properly and revealingly dedicated to Roman Jakobson, speaks eloquently of the writer's quest for a perfect coincidence of the phonic properties of a word with its signifying function. "We would also wish to insist on the Cratylism of the name (and of the sign) in Proust. . . . Proust sees the relationship between signifier and signified as motivated, the one copying the other and representing in its material form the signified essence of the thing (and not the thing itself). . . . This realism (in the scholastic sense of the word), which conceives of names as the 'copy' of the ideas, has taken, in Proust, a radical form. But one may well ask whether it is not more or less consciously present in all writing and whether it is possible to be a writer without some sort of belief in the natural relationship between names and essences. The poetic function, in the widest sense of the word, would thus be defined by a Cratylian awareness of the sign, and the writer would be the conveyor of this secular myth which wants language to imitate the idea and which, contrary to the teachings of linguistic science, thinks of signs as motivated signs."[1] To the extent that Cratylism assumes a convergence of the phenomenal aspects of language, as sound, with its signifying function as referent, it is an aesthetically oriented conception; one could, in fact, without distortion, consider aesthetic theory, including its most systematic formulation in Hegel, as the complete unfolding of the model of which the Cratylian conception of language is a version. Hegel's somewhat cryptic reference to Plato, in the *Aesthetics*, may well be interpreted in this sense. Barthes and Jakobson often seem to invite a purely aesthetic reading, yet there is a part of their statement that moves in the opposite direction. For the convergence of sound and meaning celebrated by Barthes in Proust and, as Gérard Genette has decisively shown,[2] later dismantled by Proust himself as a seductive temptation to mystified minds, is also considered here to be a mere *effect* which language can perfectly well achieve, but which bears no substantial relationship, by analogy or by ontologically grounded imitation, to anything beyond that particular effect. It is a rhetorical rather than an aesthetic function of language, an identifiable trope (paronomasis) that operates on the level of the signifier and contains no responsible pronouncement on the nature of the world — despite its powerful potential to create the opposite illusion. The phenomenality of the signifier, as sound, is unquestionably involved in the correspondence between the name and the thing named, but the link, the relationship between word and thing, is not phenomenal but conventional.

This gives the language considerable freedom from referential restraint, but it makes it epistemologically highly suspect and volatile, since its use can no longer be said to be determined by considerations of truth and falsehood, good and evil, beauty and ugliness, or pleasure and pain. Whenever this autonomous potential of language can be revealed by analysis, we are dealing with literariness and, in fact, with literature as the place where this negative knowledge about the reliability of linguistic utterance is made available. The ensuing foregrounding of material, phenomenal aspects of the signifier creates a strong illusion of aesthetic seduction at the very moment when the actual aesthetic function has been, at the very least, suspended. It is inevitable that semiology or similarly oriented methods be considered formalistic, in the sense of being aesthetically rather than semantically valorized, but the inevitability of such an interpretation does not make it less aberrant. Literature involves the voiding, rather than the affirmation, of aesthetic categories. One of the consequences of this is that, whereas we have traditionally been accustomed to reading literature by analogy with the plastic arts and with music, we now have to recognize the necessity of a non-perceptual, linguistic moment in painting and music, and learn to *read* pictures rather than to *imagine* meaning.

If literariness is not an aesthetic quality, it is also not primarily mimetic. Mimesis becomes one trope among others, language choosing to imitate a non-verbal entity just as paronomasis "imitates" a sound without any claim to identity (or reflection on difference) between the verbal and non-verbal elements. The most misleading representation of literariness, and also the most recurrent objection to contemporary literary theory, considers it as pure verbalism, as a denial of the reality principle in the name of absolute fictions, and for reasons that are said to be ethically and politically shameful. The attack reflects the anxiety of the aggressors rather than the guilt of the accused. By allowing for the necessity of a non-phenomenal linguistics, one frees the discourse on literature from naive oppositions between fiction and reality, which are themselves an offspring of an uncritically mimetic conception of art. In a genuine semiology as well as in other linguistically oriented theories, the referential function of language is not being denied — far from it; what is in question is its authority as a model for natural or phenomenal cognition. Literature is fiction not because it somehow refuses to acknowledge "reality," but because it is not *a priori* certain that language functions according to principles which are those, or which are *like* those, of the phenomenal world. It is therefore not *a priori* certain that literature is a reliable source of information about anything but its own language.

It would be unfortunate, for example, to confuse the materiality of the signifier with the materiality of what it signifies. This may seem obvious enough on the level of light and sound, but it is less so with regard to the more general phenomenality of space, time or especially of the self; no one in his right mind will try to grow grapes by the luminosity of the word "day," but it is very difficult not to conceive the pattern of one's past and future existence as in accordance with temporal and spatial schemes that belong to fictional narratives and not to the world. This does not mean that fictional narratives are not part of the world and of reality; their impact upon the world may well be all too strong for comfort. What we call ideology is precisely the confusion of linguistic with natural reality, of reference with phenomenalism. It follows that, more than any other mode of inquiry, including economics, the linguistics of literariness is a powerful and indispensable tool in the unmasking of ideological aberrations, as well as a determining factor in accounting for their occurrence. Those who reproach literary theory for being oblivious to social and historical (that is to say ideological) reality are merely stating their fear at having their own ideological mystifications exposed by the tool they are trying to discredit. They are, in short, very poor readers of Marx's *German Ideology*.

In these all too summary evocations of arguments that have been much more extensively and convincingly made by others, we begin to perceive some of the answers to the initial question: what is it about literary theory that is so threatening that it provokes such strong resistances and attacks? It upsets rooted ideologies by revealing the mechanics of their workings; it goes against a powerful philosophical tradition of which aesthetics is a prominent part; it upsets the established canon of literary works and blurs the borderlines between literary and non-literary discourse. By implication, it may also reveal the links between ideologies and philosophy. All this is ample enough reason for suspicion, but not a satisfying answer to the question. For it makes the tension between contemporary literary theory and the tradition of literary studies appear as a mere historical conflict between two modes of thought that happen to hold the stage at the same time. If the conflict is merely historical, in the literal sense, it is of limited theoretical interest, a passing squall in the intellectual weather of the world. As a matter of fact, the arguments in favor of the legitimacy of literary theory are so compelling that it seems useless to concern oneself with the conflict at all. Certainly, none of the objections to theory, presented again and again, always misinformed or based on crude misunderstandings of such terms as mimesis, fiction, reality, ideology, reference and, for that matter, relevance, can be said to be of genuine rhetorical interest.

It may well be, however, that the development of literary theory is itself overdetermined by complications inherent in its very project and unsettling with regard to its status as a scientific discipline. Resistance may be a built-in constituent of its discourse, in a manner that would be inconceivable in the natural sciences and unmentionable in the social sciences. It may well be, in other words, that the polemical opposition, the systematic non-understanding and misrepresentation, the unsubstantial but eternally recurrent objections, are the displaced symptoms of a resistance inherent in the theoretical enterprise itself. To claim that this would be sufficient reason not to envisage doing literary theory would be like rejecting anatomy because it has failed to cure mortality. The real debate of literary theory is not with its polemical opponents but rather with its own methodological assumptions and possibilities. Rather than asking why literary theory is threatening, we should perhaps ask why it has such difficulty going about its business and why it lapses so readily either into the language of self-justification and self-defense or else into the overcompensation of a programmatically euphoric utopianism. Such insecurity about its own project calls for self-analysis, if one is to understand the frustrations that attend upon its practitioners, even when they seem to dwell in serene methodological self-assurance. And if these difficulties are indeed an integral part of the problem, then they will have to be, to some extent, a-historical in the temporal sense of the term. The way in which they are encountered on the present local literary scene as a resistance to the introduction of linguistic terminology in aesthetic and historical discourse about literature is only one particular version of a question that cannot be reduced to a specific historical situation and called modern, post-modern, post-classical or romantic (not even in Hegel's sense of the term), although its compulsive way of forcing itself upon us in the guise of a system of historical periodization is certainly part of its problematic nature. Such difficulties can be read in the text of literary theory at all times, at whatever historical moment one wishes to select. One of the main achievements of the present theoretical trends is to have restored some awareness of this fact. Classical, medieval and Renaissance literary theory is now often being read in a way that knows enough about what it is doing not to wish to call itself ''modern.''

We return, then, to the original question in an attempt to broaden the discussion enough to inscribe the polemics inside the question rather than having them determine it. The resistance to theory is a resistance to the use of language about language. It is therefore a resistance to language itself or to the possibility that language contains factors or functions that cannot be reduced to intuition. But we seem to assume all too readily that, when we refer to something called "language," we know what it is we are talking about, although there is probably no word to be found in the language that is as overdetermined, self-evasive, disfigured and disfiguring as "language." Even if we choose to consider it at a safe remove from any theoretical model, in the pragmatic history of "language," not as a concept, but as a didactic assignment that no human being can bypass, we soon find ourselves confronted by theoretical enigmas. The most familiar and general of all linguistic models, the classical *trivium*, which considers the sciences of language as consisting of grammar, rhetoric, and logic (or dialectics), is in fact a set of unresolved tensions powerful enough to have generated an infinitely prolonged discourse of endless frustration of which contemporary literary theory, even at its most self-assured, is one more chapter. The difficulties extend to the internal articulations between the constituent parts as well as the articulation of the field of language with the knowledge of the world in general, the link between the *trivium* and the *quadrivium*, which covers the non-verbal sciences of number (arithmetic), of space (geometry), of motion (astronomy), and of time (music). In the history of philosophy, this link is traditionally, as well as substantially, accomplished by way of logic, the area where the rigor of the linguistic discourse about itself matches up with the rigor of the mathematical discourse about the world. Seventeenth-century epistemology, for instance, at the moment when the relationship betwen philosophy and mathematics is particularly close, holds up the language of what it calls geometry (*mos geometricus*), and which in fact includes the homogeneous concatenation between space, time and number, as the sole model of coherence and economy. Reasoning *more geometrico* is said to be "almost the only mode of reasoning that is infallible, because it is the only one to adhere to the true method, whereas all other ones are by natural necessity in a degree of confusion of which only geometrical minds can be aware."[3] This is a clear instance of the interconnection between a science of the phenomenal world and a science of language conceived as definitional logic, the pre-condition for a correct axiomatic-deductive, synthetic reasoning. The possibility of thus circulating freely between logic and mathematics has its own complex and problematic history as well as its contemporary equivalences with a different logic and a different mathematics. What matters for our present argument is that this articulation of the sciences of language with the mathematical sciences represents a particularly compelling version of a continuity between a theory of language, as logic, and the knowledge of the phenomenal world to which mathematics gives access. In such a system, the place of aesthetics is preordained and by no means alien, provided the priority of logic, in the model of the *trivium*, is not being questioned. For even if one assumes, for the sake of argument and against a great deal of historical evidence, that the link between logic and the natural sciences is secure, this leaves open the question, within the confines of the *trivium* itself, of the relationship between grammar, rhetoric and logic. And this is the point at which literariness, the use of language that foregrounds the rhetorical over the grammatical and the logical function, intervenes as a decisive but unsettling element which, in a variety of modes and aspects, disrupts the inner balance of the model and, consequently, its outward extension to the nonverbal world as well.

Logic and grammar seem to have a natural enough affinity for each other and, in the tradition of Cartesian linguistics, the grammarians of Port-Royal experienced little difficulty at being logicians as well. The same claim persists today in very different methods and terminologies that nevertheless maintain the same orientation toward the universality that logic shares with science. Replying to those who oppose the singularity of specific texts to the scientific generality of the semiotic project, A. J. Greimas disputes the right to use the dignity of "grammar" to describe a reading that would not be committed to universality. Those who have doubts about the semiotic method, he writes, "postulate the necessity of constructing a grammar for each particular text. But the essence (*le propre*) of a grammar is its ability to account for a large number of texts, and the metaphorical use of the term . . . fails to hide the fact that one has, in fact, given up on the semiotic project."[4] There is no doubt that what is here prudently called "a large number" implies the hope at least of a future model that would in fact be applicable to the generation of all texts. Again, it is not our present purpose to discuss the validity of this methodological optimism, but merely to offer it as an instance of the persistent symbiosis between grammar and logic. It is clear that, for Greimas as for the entire tradition to which he belongs, the grammatical and the logical functions of language are co-extensive. Grammar is an isotope of logic.

It follows that, as long as it remains grounded in grammar, any theory of language, including a literary one, does not threaten what we hold to be the underlying principle of all cognitive and aesthetic linguistic systems. Grammar stands in the service of logic which, in turn, allows for the passage to the knowledge of the world. The study of grammar, the first of the *artes liberales*, is the necessary pre-condition for scientific and humanistic knowledge. As long as it leaves this principle intact, there is nothing threatening about literary theory. The continuity between theory and phenomenalism is asserted and preserved by the system itself. Difficulties occur only when it is no longer possible to ignore the epistemological thrust of the rhetorical dimension of discourse, that is, when it is no longer possible to keep it in its place as a mere adjunct, a mere ornament within the semantic function.

The uncertain relationship between grammar and rhetoric (as opposed to that between grammar and logic) is apparent, in the history of the *trivium*, in the uncertain status of figures of speech or tropes, a component of language that straddles the disputed borderlines between the two areas. Tropes used to be part of the study of grammar but were also considered to be the semantic agent of the specific function (or effect) that rhetoric performs as persuasion as well as meaning. Tropes, unlike grammar, pertain primordially to language. They are text-producing functions that are not necessarily patterned on a non-verbal entity, whereas grammar is by definition capable of extra-linguistic generalization. The latent tension between rhetoric and grammar precipitates out in the problem of reading, the process that necessarily partakes of both. It turns out that the resistance to theory is in fact a resistance to reading, a resistance that is perhaps at its most effective, in contemporary studies, in the methodologies that call themselves theories of reading but nevertheless avoid the function they claim as their object.

What is meant when we assert that the study of literary texts is necessarily dependent on an act of reading, or when we claim that this act is being systematically avoided? Certainly more than the tautology that one has to have read at least some parts, however small, of a text (or read some part, however small, of a text about this text) in order to be able to make a statement about it. Common as it may be, criticism by hearsay is only rarely held up as exemplary. To stress the by no means self-evident necessity of reading implies at least two things. First of all, it implies that literature is not a transparent message in which it can be taken for granted that the distinction between the message and the means of communication is clearly established. Second, and more problematically, it implies that the grammatical decoding of a text leaves a residue of indetermination that has to be, but cannot be, resolved by grammatical means, however extensively conceived. The extension of grammar to include para-figural dimensions is in fact the most remarkable and debatable strategy of contemporary semiology, especially in the study of syntagmatic and narrative structures. The codification of contextual elements well beyond the syntactical limits of the sentence leads to the systematic study of metaphrastic dimensions and has considerably refined and expanded the knowledge of textual codes. It is equally clear, however, that this extension is always strategically directed towards the replacement of rhetorical figures by grammatical codes. This tendency to replace a rhetorical by a grammatical terminology (to speak of hypotaxis, for instance, to designate anamorphic or metonymic tropes) is part of an explicit program, a program that is entirely admirable in its intent since it tends towards the mastering and the clarification of meaning. The replacement of a hermeneutic by a semiotic model, of interpretation by decoding, would represent, in view of the baffling historical instability of textual meanings (including, of course, those of canonical texts), a considerable progress. Much of the hesitation associated with "reading" could thus be dispelled.

The argument can be made, however, that no grammatical decoding, however refined, could claim to reach the determining figural dimensions of a text. There are elements in all texts that are by no means ungrammatical, but whose semantic function is not grammatically definable, neither in themselves nor in context. Do we have to interpret the genitive in the title of Keats' unfinished epic *The Fall of Hyperion* as meaning "Hyperion's Fall," the case story of the defeat of an older by a newer power, the very recognizable story from which Keats indeed started out but from which he increasingly strayed away, or as "Hyperion Falling," the much less specific but more disquieting evocation of an actual process of falling, regardless of its beginning, its end or the identity of the entity to whom it befalls to be falling? This story is indeed told in the later fragment entitled *The Fall of Hyperion*, but it is told about a character who resembles Apollo rather than Hyperion, the same Apollo who, in the first version (called *Hyperion*), should definitely be triumphantly standing rather than falling if Keats had not been compelled to interrupt, for no apparent reason, the story of Apollo's triumph. Does the title tell us that Hyperion is fallen and that Apollo stands, or does it tell us that Hyperion and Apollo (and Keats, whom it is hard to distinguish, at times, from Apollo) are interchangeable in that all of them are necessarily and constantly falling? Both readings are grammatically correct, but it is impossible to decide from the context (the ensuing narrative) which version is the right one. The narrative context suits neither and both at the same time, and one is tempted to suggest that the fact that Keats was unable to complete either version manifests the impossibility, for him as for us, of reading his own title. One could then read the word "Hyperion" in the title *The Fall of Hyperion* figurally, or, if one wishes, intertextually, as referring not to the historical or mythological character but as referring to the title of Keats' own earlier text (*Hyperion*). But are we then telling the story of the failure of the first text as the success of the second, the Fall of *Hyperion* as the Triumph of *The Fall of Hyperion*? Manifestly, yes, but not quite, since the second text also fails to be concluded. Or are we telling the story of why all texts, as texts, can always be said to be falling? Manifestly yes, but not quite, either, since the story of the fall of the first version, as told in the second, applies to the first version only and could not legitimately be read as meaning also the fall of *The Fall of Hyperion*. The undecidability involves the figural or literal status of the proper name Hyperion as well as of the verb falling, and is thus a matter of figuration and not of grammar. In "Hyperion's Fall," the word "fall" is plainly figural, the representation of a figural fall, and we, as readers, read this fall standing up. But in "Hyperion Falling," this is not so clearly the case, for if Hyperion can be Apollo and Apollo can be Keats, then he can also be us and his figural (or symbolic) fall becomes his and our literal falling as well. The difference between the two readings is itself structured as a trope. And it matters a great deal how we read the title, as an exercise not only in semantics, but in what the text actually does to us. Faced with the ineluctable necessity to come to a decision, no grammatical or logical analysis can help us out. Just as Keats had to break off his narrative, the reader has to break off his understanding at the very moment when he is most directly engaged and summoned by the text. One could hardly expect to find solace in this "fearful symmetry" between the author's and reader's plight since, at this point, the symmetry is no longer a formal but an actual trap, and the question no longer "merely" theoretical.

This undoing of theory, this disturbance of the stable cognitive field that extends from grammar to logic to a general science of man and of the phenomenal world, can in its turn be made into a theoretical project of rhetorical analysis that will reveal the inadequacy of grammatical models of non-reading. Rhetoric, by its actively negative relationship to grammar and to logic, certainly undoes the claims of the *trivium* (and by extension, of language) to be an epistemologically stable construct. The resistance to theory is a resistance to the rhetorical or tropological dimension of language, a dimension which is perhaps more explicitly in the foreground in literature (broadly conceived) than in other verbal manifestations or — to be somewhat less vague — which can be revealed in any verbal event when it is read textually. Since grammar as well as figuration is an integral part of reading, it follows that reading will be a negative process in which the grammatical cognition is undone, at all times, by its rhetorical displacement. The model of the *trivium* contains within itself the pseudo-dialectic of its own undoing and its history tells the story of this dialectic.

This conclusion allows for a somewhat more systematic description of the contemporary theoretical scene. This scene is dominated by an increased stress on reading as a theoretical problem or, as it is sometimes erroneously phrased, by an increased stress on the reception rather than on the production of texts. It is in this area that the most fruitful exchanges have come about between writers and journals of various countries and that the most interesting dialogue has developed between literary theory and other disciplines, in the arts as well as in linguistics, philosophy and the social sciences. A straightforward *report* on the present state of literary theory in the United States would have to stress the emphasis on reading, a direction which is already present, moreover, in the New Critical tradition of the forties and the fifties. The methods are now more technical, but the contemporary interest in a poetics of literature is clearly linked, traditionally enough, to the problems of reading. And since the models that are being used certainly are no longer *simply* intentional and centered on an identifiable self, nor *simply* hermeneutic in the postulation of a single originary, pre-figural and absolute text, it would appear that this concentration on reading would lead to the rediscovery of the theoretical difficulties associated with rhetoric. This is indeed the case, to some extent; but not quite. Perhaps the most instructive aspect of contemporary theory is the refinement of the techniques by which the threat inherent in rhetorical analysis is being avoided at the very moment when the efficacy of these techniques has progressed so far that the rhetorical obstacles to understanding can no longer be mistranslated in thematic and phenomenal commonplaces. The resistance to theory which, as we saw, is a resistance to reading, appears in its most rigorous and theoretically elaborated form among the theoreticians of reading who dominate the contemporary theoretical scene.

It would be a relatively easy, though lengthy, process to show that this is so for theoreticians of reading who, like Greimas or, on a more refined level, Riffaterre or, in a very different mode, H. R. Jauss or Wolfgang Iser — all of whom have a definite, though sometimes occult, influence on literary theory in this country — are committed to the use of grammatical models or, in the case of *Rezeptionsästhetik*, to traditional hermeneutic models that do not allow for the problematization of the phenomenalism of reading and therefore remain uncritically confined within a theory of literature rooted in aesthetics. Such an argument would be easy to make because, once a reader has become aware of the rhetorical dimensions of a text, he will not be amiss in finding textual instances that are irreducible to grammar or to historically determined meaning, provided only he is willing to acknowledge what he is bound to notice. The problem quickly becomes the more baffling one of having to account for the shared reluctance to acknowledge the obvious. But the argument would be lengthy because it has to involve a textual analysis that cannot avoid being somewhat elaborate; one can succinctly suggest the grammatical indetermination of a title such as *The Fall of Hyperion,* but to confront such an undecidable enigma with the critical reception and reading of Keats' text requires some space.

The demonstration is less easy (though perhaps less ponderous) in the case of the theoreticians of reading whose avoidance of rhetoric takes another turn. We have witnessed, in recent years, a strong interest in certain elements in language whose function is not only not dependent on any form of phenomenalism but on any form of cognition as well, and which thus excludes, or postpones, the consideration of tropes, ideologies, etc., from a reading that would be primarily performative. In some cases, a link is reintroduced between performance, grammar, logic, and stable referential meaning, and the resulting theories (as in the case of Ohmann) are not in essence distinct from those of avowed grammarians or semioticians. But the most astute practitioners of a speech act theory of reading avoid this relapse and rightly insist on the necessity to keep the actual performance of speech acts, which is conventional rather than cognitive, separate from its causes and effects — to keep, in their terminology, the illocutionary force separate from its perlocutionary function. Rhetoric, understood as persuasion, is forcefully banished (like Coriolanus) from the performative moment and exiled in the affective area of perlocution. Stanley Fish, in a masterful essay, convincingly makes this point.[5] What awakens one's suspicion about this conclusion is that it relegates persuasion, which is indeed inseparable from rhetoric, to a purely affective and intentional realm and makes no allowance for modes of persuasion which are no less rhetorical and no less at work in literary texts, but which are of the order of persuasion by *proof* rather than persuasion by seduction. Thus to empty rhetoric of its epistemological impact is possible only because its tropological, figural functions are being bypassed. It is as if, to return for a moment to the model of the *trivium*, rhetoric could be isolated from the generality that grammar and logic have in common and considered as a mere correlative of an illocutionary power. The equation of rhetoric with psychology rather than with epistemology opens up dreary prospects of pragmatic banality, all the drearier if compared to the brilliance of the performative analysis. Speech act theories of reading in fact repeat, in a much more effective way, the grammatization of the *trivium* at the expense of rhetoric. For the characterization of the performative as sheer convention reduces it in effect to a grammatical code among others. The relationship between trope and performance is actually closer but more disruptive than what is here being proposed. Nor is this relationship properly captured by reference to a supposedly "creative" aspect of performance, a notion with which Fish rightly takes issue. The performative power of language can be called positional, which differs considerably from conventional as well as from "creatively" (or, in the technical sense, intentionally) constitutive. Speech act oriented theories of reading read only to the extent that they prepare the way for the rhetorical reading they avoid.

But the same is still true even if a "truly" rhetorical reading that would stay clear of any undue phenomenalization or of any undue grammatical or performative codification of the text could be conceived — something which is not necessarily impossible and for which the aims and methods of literary theory should certainly strive. Such a reading would indeed appear as the methodical undoing of the grammatical construct and, in its systematic disarticulation of the *trivium*, will be theoretically sound as well as effective. Technically correct rhetorical readings may be boring, monotonous, predictable and unpleasant, but they are irrefutable. They are also totalizing (and potentially totalitarian) for since the structures and functions they expose do not lead to the knowledge of an entity (such as language) but are an unreliable process of knowledge production that prevents all entities, including linguistic entities, from coming into discourse as such, they are indeed universals, consistently defective models of language's impossibility to be a model language. They are, always in theory, the most elastic theoretical and dialectical model to end all models and they can rightly claim to contain within their own defective selves all the other defective models of reading-avoidance, referential, semiological, grammatical, performative, logical, or whatever. They are theory and not theory at the same time, the universal theory of the impossibility of theory. To the extent however that they are theory, that is to say teachable, generalizable and highly responsive to systematization, rhetorical readings, like the other kinds, still avoid and resist the reading they advocate. Nothing can overcome the resistance to theory since theory *is* itself this resistance. The loftier the aims and the better the methods of literary theory, the less possible it becomes. Yet literary theory is not in danger of going under; it cannot help but flourish, and the more it is resisted, the more it flourishes, since the language it speaks is the language of self-resistance. What remains impossible to decide is whether this flourishing is a triumph or a fall.

Notes

1. Roland Barthes, "Proust et les noms," in *To Honor Roman Jakobson* (The Hague: Mouton, 1967), part I, pp. 157-58.

2. "Proust et le language indirect," in *Figures II* (Paris: Seuil, 1969).

3. Blaise Pascal, "De l'esprit géométrique et de l'art de persuader," in *Oeuvres complètes*, L. Lafuma, ed. (Paris: Seuil, 1963), pp. 349ff.

4. A. J. Greimas, *Du Sens* (Paris: Seuil, 1970), p. 13.

5. Stanley Fish, "How to Do Things with Austin and Searle: Speech Act Theory and Literary Criticism," in *MLN* 91 (1976), pp. 983-1025. See especially p. 1008.

The Return to Philology

The quarrelsome tone that hangs over the debates on the teaching of literature can often be traced back to the advent of contemporary literary theory. This is certainly not surprising. Whenever new approaches or techniques are being advocated, a very understandable ill-humor overcomes those who feel they may have to modify or to reconsider well-established pedagogical habits that served them well until the most recent troublemakers came along. But the polemical response in the case of contemporary theory, and especially of some of its aspects, runs deeper.

It feeds not only on civilized conservatism but on moral indignation. It speaks with an anxiety that is not only that of a disturbed tranquillity but of a disturbed moral conscience. Nor is this mood confined to the opponents of theory. Its protagonists, in most cases, are just as nervous. When they appear not to be, their self-assurance often seems to be dependent on utopian schemes. The well-established rationale for the professing of literature has come under fire. Small wonder that it chooses to shoot back.

Ever since the teaching of literature became an autonomous academic field (and we are frequently reminded that this is a fairly recent development, going back no further than the late nineteenth century) it has justified itself as a humanistic and historical discipline, allied to yet distinct from the descriptive sciences of philology and rhetoric. Its ambitions, however, go beyond mere description. It not only has its own national and comparative history but, since it deals with a relatively stable canon of specific texts, it should be a model for the other historical sciences whose subject matter is less clearly defined.

21

Moreover, it has the task of determining the meaning of texts and this hermeneutic function establishes its kinship with theology.

Finally, as a depositor of human experience of considerable variety and scope, it gains access to questions of moral philosophy — questions of value and of normative judgment. Its technical and descriptive aspects as a science of language dovetail with its historical, theological and ethical function. The professor of literature has good reasons to feel appeased; his scientific conscience is satisfied by the positive rigor of his linguistic and historical knowledge, while his moral, political and (in the extensive sense) religious conscience is assuaged by the application of this knowledge to the understanding of the world, of society and of the self. The didactics of literature could legitimately hope to be exemplary for interdisciplinary humanistic studies. Neither is this hope incompatible with literary theory and literary criticism: some forms of theory, especially those which continue a tradition of aesthetic speculation that, in the field of English, can be traced back to Coleridge, fully confirm these expectations. This would be the case for such diverse names as those of I. A. Richards, Lionel Trilling, R. P. Blackmur and Northrop Frye.

It would, however, not be quite the same for William Empson or for Kenneth Burke, or, more recently, for some, predominantly French, critics and philosophers whose work takes into account investigations pursued in the field of structural linguistics and who have kindled the ire of their humanistic colleagues. Thus, in an influential article published in the Harvard alumni bulletin, *Harvard Magazine*, September-October 1982, the Distinguished Professor of English Literature, Walter Jackson Bate, author of outstanding books on Keats, Samuel Johnson and the intellectual history of romanticism, denounced the bankruptcy of literary studies. Their increased professionalism and specialization have failed, he claims, to rescue the humanities at a time when they are said to be "in the weakest state they ever suffered — bent on a self-destructive course, through a combination of anger, fear and purblind defensiveness." In a historical overview that traces the gradual decay of literary teaching, Bate sees the increasing concentration on literary theory as the main cause for this decline. It culminates in the final catastrophe of the post-structural era, the invasion of departments of English by French influences that advocate "a nihilistic view of literature, of human communication, and of life itself."

The main culprit, denounced by name, is Jacques Derrida, said to be a "puckish Parisian" (he is neither), "who never turns to the really major philosophers except to snatch at stale pessimisms" (e.g., Nietzsche). The remark suggests that Professor Bate, a careful scholar and brilliant teacher, has this time confined his sources of information to *Newsweek* magazine.

The crisis in the teaching of literature to which Bate alerts us is genuine enough. This does not mean, however, that his diagnosis or his remedies are valid, even less so since these remedies do not take the form of a reasoned discussion but of an appeal to the administrative officers of the universities to deny tenure to teachers who concentrate on theory. The question to Bate's mind is not even in need of discussion. For all people of good will and good sense, the matter has long since been settled once and for all. What is left is a matter of law-enforcement rather than a critical debate. One must be feeling very threatened indeed to become so aggressively defensive.

My own awareness of the critical, even subversive, power of literary instruction does not stem from philosophical allegiances but from a very specific teaching experience. In the 1950s, Bate's colleague at Harvard, Reuben Brower, taught an undergraduate course in General Education entitled "The Interpretation of Literature" (better known on the Harvard campus and in the profession at large as HUM 6) in which many graduate students in English and Comparative Literature served as teaching assistants. No one could be more remote from high-powered French theory than Reuben Brower. He wrote books on Shakespeare and on Pope that are models of sensitive scholarship but not exactly manifestos for critical terrorism. He was much more interested in Greek and Latin literature than in literary theory. The critics he felt closest to, besides Eliot, were Richards and Leavis, and in both of them he was in sympathy with their emphasis on ethics.

Brower, however, believed in and effectively conveyed what appears to be an entirely innocuous and pragmatic precept, founded on Richards's "practical criticism." Students, as they began to write on the writings of others, were not to say anything that was not derived from the text they were considering. They were not to make any statements that they could not support by a specific use of language that actually occurred in the text. They were asked, in other words, to begin by reading texts closely as texts and not to move at once into the general context of human experience or history. Much more humbly or modestly, they were to start out from the bafflement that such singular turns of tone, phrase, and figure were bound to produce in readers attentive enough to notice them and honest enough not to hide their non-understanding behind the screen of received ideas that often passes, in literary instruction, for humanistic knowledge.

This very simple rule, surprisingly enough, had far-reaching didactic consequences. I have never known a course by which students were so transformed. Some never saw the point of thus restricting their attention to the matter at hand and of concentrating on the way meaning is conveyed rather than on the meaning itself. Others, however, caught on very quickly and, henceforth, they would never be the same. The papers they handed in at the end of the course bore little resemblance to what they produced at the beginning. What they lost in generality, they more than made up for in precision and in the closer proximity of their writing to the original mode. It did not make writing easier for them for they no longer felt free to indulge in any thought that came into their head or to paraphrase any idea they happened to encounter. The profession is littered with the books that the students of Reuben Brower failed to write. Good readers often are spare writers and in the present state of literary studies, that is all to the good.

Here was a course, then, utterly devoid of subversive intentions as well as of theoretical objections. The conceptual and terminological apparatus was kept to a minimum, with only a few ordinary language terms for metalanguage. The entire stance was certainly not devoid of its own ideological and methodological assumptions, yet they managed to remain implicit without interfering with the procedures. Reuben Brower had a rare talent, not out of respect for the delicacy of language, for keeping things as tidy as a philosophical investigation ought to be yet, at the same time, entirely pragmatic. Mere reading, it turns out, prior to any theory, is able to transform critical discourse in a manner that would appear deeply subversive to those who think of the teaching of literature as a substitute for the teaching of theology, ethics, psychology, or intellectual history. Close reading accomplishes this often in spite of itself because it cannot fail to respond to structures of language which it is the more or less secret aim of literary teaching to keep hidden.

Attention to the philological or rhetorical devices of language is not the same as aesthetic appreciation, although the latter can be a way of access to the former. Perhaps the most difficult thing for students and teachers of literature to realize is that their appreciation is measured by the analytical rigor of their own discourse about literature, a criterion that is not primarily or exclusively aesthetic. Yet it separates the sheep from the goats, the consumers from the *professors* of literature, the chit-chat of evaluation from actual perception.

The personal experience of Reuben Brower's Humanities 6 was not so different from the impact of theory on the teaching of literature over the past ten or fifteen years. The motives may have been more revolutionary and the terminology was certainly more intimidating. But, in practice, the turn to theory occurred as a return to philology, to an examination of the structure of language prior to the meaning it produces. This is so even among the most controversial French theoreticians. Foucault's first major book, *Les mots et les choses*, as its title indicates, has to do with the referential relationship between language and reality, but it approaches the question not in terms of philosophical speculation but, much more pragmatically, as it appears in the methodological innovations of social scientists and philologists. Whereas Derrida's starting point, though more traditionally "philosophical" in appearance, stresses the empirical powers of language over those of intuition and knowledge. His critique of phenomenology in the name of linguistics, by way of Husserl and Saussure, bears this out. Even in the case of Nietzsche, a frequent point of reference for all these writers, the accent falls on Nietzsche the philologist rather than on Nietzsche the existential nihilist.

Why, then, the cries of doom and the appeals to mobilization against a common enemy? It appears that the return to philology, whether it occurs casually or as a consequence of highly self-conscious, philosophical mutations, upsets the taken-for-granted assumptions with which the profession of literature has been operating. As a result, the attribution of a reliable, or even exemplary, cognitive and, by extension, ethical function to literature indeed becomes much more difficult. But this is a recurrent philosophical quandary that has never been resolved. The latest version of the question, which still determines our present-day convictions about the aims of literature, goes back to the rise of aesthetics as an independent discipline in the later half of the eighteeneth century. The link between literature (as art), epistemology, and ethics is the burden of aesthetic theory at least since Kant. It is because we teach literature as an aesthetic function that we can move so easily from literature to its apparent prolongations in the spheres of self-knowledge, of religion, and of politics.

In its origin and its development, aesthetics has been the province of philosophers of nature and of the self rather than of philosophers of language. Neither has aesthetic theory succeeded in its admirable ambition to unite cognition, desire and morality in one single synthetic judgment. Professor Bate, in the article mentioned before, asserts as a matter of course that it suffices to "turn to Kant" to lay to rest a linguistically motivated scepticism like that of David Hume. He echoes a generally admitted position among professors of literature rather than among professors of philosophy.

Whether a reading of *The Critique of Judgment*, as distinct from its simplified versions in Schiller and his offspring, would confirm this assertion certainly stands in need of careful examination. Contemporary literary theory has started this long overdue process.

Literary theory raises the unavoidable question whether aesthetic values can be compatible with the linguistic structures that make up the entities from which these values are derived. Such questions never ceased to haunt the consciousness of writers and philosophers. They come to the fore in the ambivalent rejection of rhetoric at the very moment that it was being used and refined as never before, or in the assimilation of the considerable aesthetic charge emanating from rhetorical tropes to the aesthetic neutrality of grammar. It is by no means an established fact that aesthetic values and linguistic structures are incompatible. What is established is that their compatibility, or lack of it, has to remain an open question and that the manner in which the teaching of literature, since its beginning in the later nineteenth century, has foreclosed the question is unsound, even if motivated by the best of intentions. What also ought to be (but is not) established is that the professing of literature ought to take place under the aegis of this question.

From a purely methodological point of view, this would not be difficult to achieve. It would involve a change by which literature, instead of being taught only as a historical and humanistic subject, should be taught as a rhetoric and a poetics prior to being taught as a hermeneutics and a history. The institutional resistances to such a move, however, are probably insurmountable. For one thing, it changes departments of English from being large organizations in the service of everything except their own subject matter into much smaller units, dedicated to the professional specialization that Professor Bate deplores. It also requires a change in the rationale for the teaching of literature, away from standards of cultural excellence that, in the last analysis, are always based on some form of religious faith, to a principle of disbelief that is not so much scientific as it is critical, in the full philosophical sense of the term. One sees easily enough why such changes are not likely to occur.

Yet, with the critical cat now so far out of the bag that one can no longer ignore its existence, those who refuse the crime of theoretical ruthlessness can no longer hope to gain a good conscience. Neither, of course, can the theorists — but, then, they never laid claim to it in the first place.

Hypogram and Inscription

As seen from the public perspective of literary journalists and literary critics, the disputes among literary theorists more and more appear to be like quarrels among theologians, at the furthest remove from any reality or practicality. It is harder than ever, on these battlefields, to tell friend from foe, more difficult still to state the issues in intelligible ordinary language. One feels tempted to stress the existence of a dividing line between the marketplace and the monastery, between the public arena and the academy, by pointing out that there is nothing whatever in common between the discourses held in either place. But the validity of such a dividing line will soon enough become itself the divisive issue. Disputes among theologians, for all their abstruseness, have in fact very public equivalents; how is one to separate the disputations between nominalists and realists in the fourteenth century from "the waning of the Middle Ages"? Perhaps the fine, nearly imperceptible line that, in the present day, separates semioticians and grammarians from theoreticians of rhetoric — a line that frequently traverses one and the same author's work — may be inextricably intertwined with the "waning" of modernity. Whatever the case may be, such a line, if it exists, is not easy to trace. The similarities and oppositions that appear on the surface and that determine institutional groupings and complicities are often more confusing than revealing, and the passage from the sociology of literary theory as an academic institution to the actual theoretical issues is clogged by so many false mediations as to be nearly impassable.

It is not true, however, that the secluded discourse of "pure" speculation and scholarship is entirely distinct from the public discourse of controversy, less

27

true still that the one is unilaterally sound while the other is chaotic, or that the one is free from the ideology that animates and distorts the other. Patterns of obfuscation and of lucidity inhabit both and the homologies between these patterns can be organized around shared assumptions, however diversely they may be valorized.

Few theoreticians of literature seem more remote from public controversy than Michael Riffaterre. His work is like that of a scientist or, rather, of a technician addressing other technicians; his polemics can be very pointed, but they involve fellow specialists whose theoretical assumptions are quite close to his own, rather than ideologues or philosophers. A terse and economic writer in the best classical tradition, he is certainly not given to large pronouncements on life, death, or the state of the world. One reads his masterful, witty, learned and altogether enlightened papers with considerable pleasure, but it is like the pleasure one derives from a drawing by Ingres, say, rather than from *Le Radeau de la Méduse*. No world-shaking events or pronouncements are being recorded, only a small detail in the structure of the universe being appreciated or corrected — as well as a great deal of potential bombast and stupidity avoided. Even from a methodological point of view, such terms as *breakthrough* or *discoveries* are not the first to come to mind in characterizing the work of this lucid analyst. Yet he has succeeded in challenging constructively some of the most powerful theoretical constructs in linguistic theory and, in the process, developed what is probably the most reliable didactic model for the teaching of literature, regardless of period or language, available at the present. Still, for all its genuine modesty of purpose and for all its deliberate confinement to technical specialization, the work of Riffaterre, more than is generally noticed, occupies a prominent place in philosophical debates whose magnitude transcends the pragmatic discrepancies between public and academic discourse.

It is not Riffaterre's intention thus to become more publicly exposed. Indeed, such a claim made for the wider philosophical significance of his writings goes, to some degree, against the premises and the conclusions of these very writings. Such, however, is the power of things linguistic that, whenever a mind has the strength to reach into their proximity, it finds itself at once projected into regions which, though less ephemeral than those of public polemics, are also more crowded and less serene than those of pure speculation.

The didactic effectiveness of Riffaterre's method is more than a convenient starting point for the discussion of its *enjeu théorique*. If this paper were to be an evaluation rather than an attempt at understanding, one would have to linger over the extent and the quality of this success, now widely acknowledged here and abroad. But the very success raises at once the question of the relationship between the didactics and the theory of literary language: what is implied, for theory, in such perfect compatibility between theory and teaching? Is the didactic productivity the reward, so to speak, for the accuracy of the theory, or is it the compensation, or the excuse, for certain theoretical foreclosures? It may not be easy to answer this question in a decisive manner, for the relationship between the truth-value of a theoretical inquiry and the exemplarity of the resulting pedagogy, the relationship, in other words, between *Wahrheit* and *Methode*, is not simply complementary — nor is it simply antithetical or symmetrical in any other way. To dissociate the didactic strength of a method entirely from its epistemological consistency would be absurd: in theory, a theory that is true to its object lends itself better, in the long run, to being taught than one that is not; no amount of browbeating or of seduction can hide forever a flaw of reason. Yet this proposition raises more questions than can be dealt with, especially when the ''object'' of the theory is linguistic, let alone literary. Even in the field of mathematics and the natural sciences, the question is not simple, as is evident from the recurrence of unresolved philosophical quandaries that have proliferated around it: whether teaching should be the product of logic or of dialectics, whether it involves analytic or synthetic judgments, etc.[1] In the field of the historical and linguistic sciences, some new problems are added while the old ones are not allowed to disappear. It is not at all certain, for instance, that the practical results of the theory, the manner in which it allows one to carry out specific assignments and to read specific texts, can be detached from the theoretical investigation itself and thus made available to those who have not actually taken part in this investigation. The problem seems to be entirely mastered in Riffaterre's own work, in which the theory and the reading sustain each other and are made to dovetail with the skill of a master craftsman. Yet, again, the suspicion must then arise that perhaps the theory is being controlled by this pragmatic aim rather than by the necessities inherent in its object. The spirit of rational inquiry owes it to itself to be especially wary of the didactic successes to which it is committed; that Michael Riffaterre's work is inspired by this spirit is clear from the insistence with which it reiterates its determination to resist aspects of its own results that might widen the gap between the theory and the *paideia* of literature.

The main theoretical difficulty inherent in the teaching of literature is the delimitation of borderlines that circumscribe the literary field by setting it apart from other modes of discourse. Hence the nervousness which any tampering with the canonical definition of a literary corpus is bound to provoke. In a manner that is more acute for theoreticians of literature than for theoreticians of the natural or the social world, it can be said that they do not quite know what it is they are talking about, not only in the metaphysical sense that the whatness, the ontology of literature is hard to fathom, but also in the more elusive sense that, whenever one is supposed to speak of literature, one speaks of anything under the sun (including, of course, oneself) except literature. The need for determination thus becomes all the stronger as a way to safeguard a discipline which constantly threatens to degenerate into gossip, trivia or self-obsession. The most traditional term to designate these borderlines is "form"; in literature, the concept of form is, before anything else, a definitional necessity. No literary metadiscourse would ever be conceivable in its absence. Before berating a critic or a thoretician for his formalism, one should realize that it is the necessary precondition to any theory. This does not mean, however, that the concept of form is itself susceptible of definition.

Riffaterre is a declared, impenitent, and consequential formalist and he states his conviction in the most traditional of terms as "the triumph, in poetry, of form over content," as the assimilation of poetic texts to "monuments" as well as to "games," and as a clear separation between the language of poetry and what he calls the "linear" language of cognition and of mimetic speech, in which words are supposed to correspond to things.[2] The separation extends to the language of literary analysis, which is self-effacing, scrupulous and restricted, and the invention of literary composition: the agrammaticality of the literary text is not tolerated in the commentary.[3] A dogmatic discussion of these dogmatic assertions will be of no avail in describing our author's contribution. By stating them, as he does, in the blandest and most apodictic of terms, he makes their heuristic function evident. An eventual critique will have to consider the results which these postulates allow one to reach rather than their merit as transcendental judgments. Moreover, the postulates of poetic formalism are by no means far-fetched or paradoxical; they are, in fact, so overwhelmingly self-evident that the problem becomes not so much why the notion of poetry as a non-referential discourse can be asserted, but rather why it is resisted to such an extent that even as radical a formalist as Riffaterre has to account for the resistance. Nor should one too hastily decide to valorize the act of appropriation implied in establishing these borderlines. One tends to look upon it as a fastidious attempt to keep literature sheltered from the rough-and-tumble of the "real" world. But enclosures or borderlines function in at least two directions. One may indeed want to keep the rabble away from the sacred monument one is privileged to inhabit; monuments, however, are also highly public places, known to attract squatters and miscellaneous citizens not necessarily motivated by reverence, and one might want to protect what lies beyond the realm of the poetic from the shameful goings on that occur within its boundaries. For all its monumentality, Riffaterre's "form" is anything but stodgy, nor is it free from the trickeries Freud discovers in jokes and in dreams. He just possibly might want to protect the rational world from poetry's bad example.

All formalistic theories of poetry sooner or later have to confront a similar problem: their adequation to the phenomenally realized aspects of their topic makes them highly effective as a descriptive discipline, but at the cost of understanding. A monument, per definition, is self-sufficient; it can at most be contemplated but it exists quite independently of its beholder, even and especially when it houses his mortal remains. Formalism, in other words, can only produce a stylistics (or a poetics) and not a hermeneutics of literature, and it remains deficient in trying to account for the relationship between these two approaches. Yet a formalist like Riffaterre feels compelled to integrate the hermeneutic activity of the reader within his enterprise. How can he hope to accomplish this without undoing the postulate of self-referentiality which defines and delimits for him the specificity of literature? In saying this, we have evoked the dynamics of Riffaterre's work as it moves from the *Essais de stylistique structurale* (published in 1971 but also containing articles written almost ten years earlier) to the recent *Semiotics of Poetry* (1978). The precision and the resourcefulness of his analyses make him into a model case for examining if and how the poetics of literary form can be made compatible with the hermeneutics of reading. More is at stake in this than the didactics of literary instruction or the possibility of literary history; at stake, first and foremost, is the category of the aesthetic as guardian of the rational cognition it appears to subvert and, beyond this, the destiny of cognition itself as it runs the risk of having to confront texts without the shelter of aesthetic distance.

The shift from *stylistics* to *semiotics* in the titles of Riffaterre's main theoretical books designates a genuine change, or variation, in the theoretical subtext of his method. He always remained quite independent of prevailing trends, but his earlier work could be called similar to that of the Russian Formalists in that it describes already elaborated codes and structures rather than trying to analyze the (infra)-structures that explain the possibility of their elaboration. In his stylistics, literary language functions as a paradigmatic sign which generates its own sign systems, but no attempt is made to analyze structurally the sign-character, the semioticity of the stylistic marker as such. Stylistics, in other words, is in Riffaterre's own formulation of the distinction, a semiology, not a semiotics. As such it would not, in all rigor, have to consider the function of the reader at all, for the mere description of the encoding system that constitutes the text will correspond, point by point and exhaustively, to the form. The *décryptage* or decoding is pre-determined and saturates the field of signification without meeting obstacles that could not be overcome by acquired skills. As is also the case, for very different reasons, in onto-theological hermeneutics, the sole purpose of reading is to do away with reading entirely. In a strictly formalistic system, reading is at most a clearing away of the referential and ideological rubble, prior to the undertaking of the descriptive analysis. Reading is a contingent and not a structural part of the form.

Yet, even in the *Essais de stylistique structurale*, Riffaterre was never willing to endorse the elimination of reading that stylistics implies. One can instead see his entire enterprise as a sustained theoretical effort to integrate reading into the formal description of the text without exploding its borders. Thus, in the polemical exchange with Roman Jakobson about the latter's interpretation, in collaboration with Claude Lévi-Strauss, of Baudelaire's poem "Les Chats," an article which dates from the mid-sixties, Riffaterre repeatedly insists on the necessity for any method of analysis to correspond to the actual reading experience of the text. It is not enough for the textual significance[4] to be actualized in the language (for example in grammatical or lexical structures); for the significance to be poetic it has to be actualized in the process that takes place between text and reader. The grammatical structures singled out by Jakobson and Lévi-Strauss are irrelevant because "they do not explain what establishes the contact between the poetry and the reader" (*Stylistique*, p. 325). Riffaterre's own version of Baudelaire's text postulates that "the nature of the poetic phenomenon" implies reading, a reading cleansed of referential aberrations but a reading all the same. It even stages the composite persona of a super-reader who "possesses the considerable advantage of following the normal process of reading, of perceiving the poem as it is imposed on us by its linguistic configuration, by following the sentence, starting out at the beginning . . ." (p. 327). And, in a later addition to the original text, Riffaterre returns to the point: "One will never insist enough on the importance of a reading that proceeds in the same direction as the text, namely from the start to the finish. If one fails to respect this 'one way street,' one disregards an essential element of the literary phenomenon . . . namely, that the text is the object of a gradual discovery, of a dynamic and constantly changing perception, in which the reader not only moves from surprise to surprise but sees, as he moves forward, his own understanding of what he has read being modified, each new finding adding a new dimension to previous elements that are being repeated, or contradicted, or expanded . . . " (p. 327).

What matters in this quotation is the stress on reading rather than on sequence. The latter is in fact a possible remnant of the line-by-line explication that used to be practiced in French *lycées*, and it is to a large extent aberrant. For it is not true that the first or the recapitulative perception of a reader is sequential at all, especially in the case of a lyric poem. Nor is it true that such a reading develops dramatically as a series of reversals and anagnorises. Such concepts belong to the linear world of Aristotelian mimesis from which Riffaterre is anxious to distance himself in all other respects. Nor do they correspond to the impact on the reader of a text whose principle of articulation is primarily mnemonic rather than dramatic, coded, that is, to being learned by heart. There are no later examples, as far as I know, in Riffaterre's work of the somewhat tedious procedure that mars his counter-commentary of "Les Chats," divided into enumerative sub-sections and flattened out, in each section, by the constraint of a non-existent sequentiality. Metaphors for the motion of reading proposed by him at a later date, such as "scanning," are a great deal more accurate. The point, however, is of limited theoretical import. For what matters most to Riffaterre is the necessity for textual actualization and, more specifically, for actualization as reading.[5] The reader-oriented procedure remains a theoretical invariant throughout his work.

One could speculate at length on the reasons and the influences that prompted an orientation which complicates and enriches his theoretical position to a considerable degree. It may well have been the feeling of liberation felt by any European-trained interpreter of literature transposed to America in the late forties and discovering that close reading could be the most challenging part of any commentary, more challenging than the historical and philological information from which it cannot be dissociated, and than the thematic paraphrase which it tends to render superfluous. Books such as I. A. Richards' *Practical Criticism* or Empson's *Seven Types of Ambiguity*, not to mention their New Critical extensions, never left the slightest trace on French literary studies. It is no exaggeration to say that, with very few and entirely non-academic exceptions,[6] French literary criticism developed and flourished by bypassing the question of reading altogether. Up till very recently, French critics never bothered to read at all, or never considered the problem worthy of their attention — which did not prevent them from writing abundantly, and often with considerable perspicacity, about texts they did not read. This was obviously so, for different reasons, for the traditions of Sainte-Beuve, of Taine, of Brunetière and of Lanson, but it was still true of thematic critics such as Poulet, Richard and, to a degree, Blanchot, in the forties and the fifties: all of them treat language, in its function as carrier of subjective experience, as if it were transparent. The same is still by and large the case for Barthes and his continuators; the only French theoretician who actually *reads* texts, in the full theoretical sense of the term, is Jacques Derrida. Riffaterre's orientation toward reader reception makes him an "American" rather than a "French" critic, or at least one of those who have helped to strip these national labels of some of their still considerable power of mystification. Thus, in a communication to a 1969 meeting at UCLA entitled "French Formalism" (now included, in a French version, in *Stylistique*) Riffaterre offered a critique of Barthes and of the *Tel Quel* authors of the period[7] in which he praises their emancipation from the tyranny of referential literalism but chides them for "masking the modalities of the perception of the literary message" (*Stylistique*, p. 268) by ignoring the reader's participation in this perception. Perception is indeed the right term, for Riffaterre has consistently held to the position that it is not sufficient for a poetic significance to be latent or erased, but that it must be manifest, actualized in a way that allows the analyst to point to a specific, determined textual feature which he can localize and which, in its turn, determines or overdetermines the response of the reader. In the absence of such evidence, the commentator as well as the reader would be open to the wildest arbitrariness. When one then asks what the condition is for a textual significant to be actualized, the answer is at least twofold. It has, first of all, to attract attention by anomaly, by what Riffaterre calls its agrammaticality, its deviation from the expectations of "ordinary" mimesis: when Hugo, for example, makes a shield behave as if it were an offensive weapon that knocks down an opponent as with a club

(*Production*, p. 195), then this anomaly, far from being evidence of casual or sloppy writing, marks a moment at which one shifts from a referential to a poetic code, and it provides the analyst with a symptom from which he can identify one of the transformational systems at work in the text. The agrammatical signal can take on a variety of forms: it can be lexical, grammatical, syntactical, figural, or intratextual, but whatever the linguistic mode may be, its actuality is always determined by its phenomenality, by its accessibility to intuition or cognition. If this is not the case, Riffaterre denies it any significance. The French novelist and occasional theoretician Ricardou is reproved for claiming to discover the anagram "gold" in Poe's phrase "right h*old*ing" despite the fact that the "g" in "right" is not sounded in English. Whatever one may think of Ricardou's plays or anagrams, Riffaterre's objection is based on a more general principle: the inaudible "g," like Jakobson and Lévi-Strauss's unimaginable constellations, is not considered to be actualized because it possesses no phenomenal reality. It is not accessible to the senses, either directly or, in the case of a visual rather than an auditive effect, by means of figuration. The criterion for actualization is no longer referential (one is not supposed to assume that the word corresponds to the thing named) but it is still phenomenal. The mark, or signal, of the anomaly still derives from representation as its negation. The transfer from referent to signifier occurs without loss of the phenomenal substance of the sign; one might even say that it is enhanced and that the poetic reader has better literal ears and better imaginative eyes than the referential one. The "symbolist" valorizations remain intact. One can claim auditive effects such as rhyme and alliteration to be actualizations since spoken language has a phenomenal existence as sound or as voice. But this same spoken language possesses, of course, no visual phenomenality whatever and all transpositions from sound into image are figural. Imaginative figuration implies that the articulation of the sign with its signification occurs by means of a structure that is itself phenomenally realized, that is to say it treats the sign as if it were fundamentally a symbol. Riffaterre seems to avoid this cluster of problems, which makes up the traditional problematics of aesthetic theory, by assimilating, through the mediation of the reader, phenomenal intuition to semantic cognition; even in his stylistic (as distinguished from his semiotic) period, the structural unit is a semantic unit of meaning. As we know from Kant, and as is certainly not openly contested by Hegel, this interiorization of intuition as meaning is entirely compatible with the phenomenalism of aesthetic experience. In his insistence on actualization, Riffaterre repeats the perennial and necessary gesture which founds the category of the aesthetic as a confirmation of the phenomenality of language. Whenever this phenomenality is being contested — and it always is — aesthetics, in one of its numberless guises, comes to the rescue. In our present-day historical configuration, this strategy is at work in the complex oppositions and complicities that develop between phenomenological and semiotic theories of language, between Husserl and Saussure. In the case of Riffaterre, whose references are literary rather than philosophical, the interplay could be said to occur between, for example, the aesthetic formalism of Paul Valéry and the semiotic irreverence of the surrealists.

What is implied, then, when the "French formalists" are criticized for neglecting the response of the reader, is that they have gone astray in their suspension of the referential function of poetic texts by allowing it to compromise the phenomenal and cognitive experience of reading. If the phenomenality of the text is allowed to disappear, there remains literally nothing left to be read. Riffaterre seems quite secure in the defense of his brand of stylistics against the semiotic overkill of his compatriots: the actualization of signification is what allows the text to be read and the possibility of reading certifies the necessity of this actualization. The argument is circular but it is a circle supported by a lengthy and respectable tradition. Nevertheless, this is also the moment when Riffaterre starts to move away from the vocabulary of stylistics and to emphasize semiotic terminology and procedures. Since his theoretical moves are at no time dictated by expediency, one can assume that he was responding to actual or potential objections that required some adjustments in the theoretical model.

Indeed, the theory of textual actualization and the theory of reader response, in the *Essais de stylistique structurale*, are not as clearly coextensive as they should be. The necessity for reading is justified in two not entirely compatible ways. On the one hand, reading is a guided response to the strict determination of the textual markers, and, as such, it is a stable process that can be accomplished with a great deal of hermeneutic self-confidence, the theoretically justified and therefore entirely legitimate assurance one hears in Riffaterre's tone when he engages specific texts. But, on the other hand, it is a dialectic born from a necessary error called "the presumption of reference": "therefore, although poetry is centered in words rather than in things, the reader, conditioned by the constant use of referential language, rationalizes as if there were a reference. He is like Alice listening to *Jabberwocky* . . ." (*Stylistique*, p. 268). Or, in an even more pointed formulation: ". . . the comparison of the poem with reality is a critical approach of dubious effectiveness: it leads to irrelevant conclusions, for it falls outside or short of the text. However, even if the recourse to reality is an inexcusable rationalization on the part of the critic, this same rationalization is one of the modalities of the relationship between text and reader which constitutes the literary phenomenon. It will therefore be necessary to try to account for it" (*Production*, p. 176). The agrammaticalities which direct the reader with such a steady hand also and at the same time grievously misguide him. And both functions are equally important: "The mechanics of the presumption of reference play as capital a part in the literary phenomenon as does the absence of reference that starts them off. The terrain remains unexplored" (*Stylistique*, p. 289). The explanations offered fail, however, to begin this necessary exploration. They assume, among other things, a separation between the smart critic and the naive reader that is out of character in an author who has a healthy respect for the "natural" reader and for the communal diction of clichés. To say that one reads referentially because one is "conditioned" to perform what is also called an "inexcusable" aberration fails to do justice to a much more baffling problem. Popular, non-academic readers or writers are often much better than professional critics at preserving the delicate and ever-suspended balance between reference and play that is the condition for aesthetic pleasure; as an instance among many, Barthes' considerations on mass cultural events in his *Mythologies* help to dispel the notion of a conditioned referentialism. The "constant use of referential language" is an invention of bad teachers of literature, a group among which Riffaterre emphatically does not belong and for which he reserves his most deadly polemical shafts.

But the question remains: what is one to make of this guided misguided reading? The practice of the early as well as the later Riffaterre is never purely corrective, confined to the dispelling of referential delusions. It always includes a powerfully positive element that reveals formal structures at the very core of the semiosis, without having to isolate artificially properties of meter and sound from the signifying function of the text. At this point in his theoretical speculation, Riffaterre's theoretical model seems to lag somewhat behind his praxis. The need to overcome the discrepancy, stimulated no doubt by the general development of semiotics here and abroad, took him back to the beginnings of this science in Peirce and especially in Saussure. Announced in a footnote to the article on the French formalists (*Stylistique*, pp. 270-271, note 25), the theory of the textual paragram and hypogram, concepts that stem from Saussure, will become the theoretical crux of Riffaterre's work from 1971 on. It constitutes the theoretical substructure of *Semiotics of Poetry* and receives systematic treatment in several essays, up to the present.

It is the Saussure of the anagrams that reawakened a strong interest among theorists, including Riffaterre, in the early seventies.[8] With good reason, for Saussure's conviction, or strong hunch, that Latin poetry was structured by the coded dispersal (or dissemination) of an underlying word or proper name throughout the lines of verse substitutes a process of formal elaboration for a referential reading. For someone like Riffaterre, who had consistently argued for the suspension, in poetry, of the referential function, the hypothesis is both a confirmation and a new possibility. It is however also potentially disruptive to the highest degree; one knows that Saussure himself backed away from it and had abandoned his investigations by the time he started to deliver the lectures that lead to the *Cours de linguistique générale*. The potential drama of this most private and inconspicuous of revolutions (including its assumed suppression by its discoverer, as if Columbus had decided to keep his discovery of the New World to himself) has acquired a certain mythological quality among contemporary theoreticians.

For Saussure's caution supports the assumption of a terror glimpsed. As is well known, he claims to have interrupted his inquiries partly because he could find no historical evidence for the existence of the elaborate codes he had reconstructed, but principally because he could not prove whether the structures were random, the outcome of mere probability, or determined by the codification of a semiosis. Riffaterre, whose commitment to determination is very strong, feels the challenge of this predicament and uses it as the starting point for the adjustment of his own text-theory. In the process, however, what was probably Saussure's most disturbing supposition gets displaced in a manner that is both very productive hermeneutically and very effective as a defense.

As is also well known, Saussure hesitated a great deal in his choice of a terminology by which to designate the distribution of the verbal unit which, he firmly believed, underlay the texts on which he was working. He considered "anagram," then stated a preference for "paragram," which implies no restriction in the space over which the key word is dispersed. Elsewhere, he stated his preference for "hypogram"(sub-text or, better, infra-text) which, as Sylvère Lotringer convincingly shows, recaptures the unity of the word as master-word or name. All these terms, whatever the differences between them, always use the suffix *gram* (letter) rather than *phone* (sound) yet, insists Saussure: "Neither anagram nor paragram [nor, we can infer, hypogram] mean that the figures of poetry are directed by way of written signs; but to replace -gram by -phone in one or each of these words would probably lead one to think that some unheard of, monstrous species of things are involved" (*Mots*, p. 31). The "choses inouie[s]" would precisely be that the phonic, sensory and phenomenal ground of poetic diction has been unsettled, for the laws for the dispersal of the key word in the text, be it as ana-, para-, or hypogram, are not phenomenally nor even mathematically perceivable. Since the key word is the proper name in all its originary integrity, its subdivision into discrete parts and groups resembles, on the level of meaning, the worst phantasms of dismemberment to be found in D. P. Schreber's *Denkwürdigkeiten eines Nervenkranken*. We would then have witnessed, in effect, the undoing of the phenomenality of language which always entails (since the phenomenal and the noumenal are binary poles within the same system) the undoing of cognition and its replacement by the uncontrollable power of the letter as inscription.[9] By choosing the word *hypogram*, yet making it function as a voiceable name rather than as an inscription, Saussure shelters language from a cognitive dismemberment which it takes a certain degree of naiveté to celebrate as the beneficial surplus-value of a gratified desire. The stakes, indeed, are quite considerable. Rather than a "mere" repression (as Lotringer would have it, and by way of Hegel, to boot), Saussure's retheorization of the question in the *Cours* can more charitably be seen as the insistence of theoretical discourse in the face of the dangers it reveals. As Derrida was able to show in *De la grammatologie*, without having recourse to the then still largely unpublished *cahiers*,[10] the *Cours de linguistique générale* is anything but an authoritatively monolithic text.

Riffaterre's transformation of Saussure's unexemplary model seems slight enough: in the space of one or two brief passages[11] he makes the hypogram into a hypotext. The fragmentation of Saussure's key-word into syllable-pairs (and potentially into letters) is replaced by the hypothesis of an underlying key-text, which is not a word, still less an inscription, but a "donnée sémantique," a unit of readable meaning susceptible of grammatical predication, but not privileged in any way as to its semantic *value*.[12] The function of the textual elaboration is not, however, to *state* this meaning (which would be devoid of all interest since there is nothing remarkable about the semantic kernel) but rather to hide it, as Saussure's key-word is hidden in the lines of verse, or, rather, to disguise it into a system of variations or paragrams which have been overdetermined by codification in such a manner as to tantalize the reader into a self-rewarding process of discovery. "The hypograms . . . are either pointed to by textual signs or are fragmentarily actualized" (*Semiotics*, p. 165). For although the hypogram behaves coyly enough, it will eventually be unveiled since this is, in fact, its *raison d'être*: the form is encoded in such a way as to reveal its own principle of determination. As the genuine practical critic that he is, Riffaterre's main interest focuses on the mechanics of dissimulation rather than on the discussion of the theoretical model. And it is certainly in the analysis of these mechanics as they occur in specific texts that he celebrates his principal triumphs, especially when (as is often the case, though it is not a theoretical necessity) the determinations occur by means of intertexts within the literary canon which he dominates to perfection. Every reader will have his own favorite *trouvaille* from among the rich harvest that Riffaterre's erudition and highly trained ear allow him to gather. Riffaterre himself, I surmise, is probably the happiest when he can detect and identify the Virgilian hypograms that structure the system of French poetry from Hugo to surrealism; the fact that the citations from Virgil are most often grammatical examples culled from textbooks used in the French *lycées* should be particularly satisfying, since it underscores that the virtue of the hypogram is certainly not its semantic "depth" but rather its grammatical resourcefulness. In Riffaterre's very convincing view of canonical literary history, Virgil has, for Baudelaire or for Hugo, a function close to that of Diabelli's little waltz theme for Beethoven.

Riffaterre's reader now has acquired a double but well-integrated task. Altered by the mimetic anomalies, he sets out on his quest for the hidden hypogram and is, up to a point, rewarded with its discovery — with the important proviso that, in this case, getting there is definitely much more than half the fun. What is finally revealed can, as in dreams interpreted by Freud, seem very little compared to the intricacy of the work that was needed to disguise it. It can, in fact, be nothing at all. Yet its existence, actual or potential, is indispensable for the entire process to take place. The reader decrypts and tentatively unveils until, as Riffaterre puts it, he "is reconverted to proper reading when the structural equivalences become apparent all at once, in a blaze of revelation" (*Semiotics*, p. 166).

What Riffaterre has done is to re-lexicalize Saussure, and no amount of emphasis on the mechanics of the procedure will undo the weight of this gesture. He may insist repeatedly on the purely verbal quality of a hypotext which is, in essence, not more than an example-sentence in a grammatical textbook, but the principle that makes the hypogram into a text, the matrix, if one wishes, of the hypogrammatic system is the determined, stable principle of meaning in its full phenomenal and cognitive sense. As such, it contains, in literature, the possibility of the negation of this affirmation. At the limit, repeating the structure of which they are abyssal versions, all the hypograms and matrixes say the same thing: they meaningfully repeat the suspension of meaning that defines literary form. All verse is nonsense verse, but nonsense verse that knows itself to be such: "the *donnée* is thus . . . the process of referential negation. But a text which proclaims the non-existence of the referent is only an extreme form of the literary discourse" (*Production*, p. 88). At this evolved stage in the development of the theoretical model, we rediscover the formal postulate from which we started out; we in fact never left the field of formalist stylistics and the detour through semiotics has been an assimilation of semiotics to stylistics rather than the reverse.

At this point, it is equally clear that the sharp original distinction between, on the one hand, linear, mimetic, and discursive language and, on the other, poetic non-referentiality is overcome. Both are mirror images of each other which do not threaten the fundamental oneness of language as a meaning-producing function. Literature is a variant within an invariant system of meaning, the extreme variant of "diametrical opposition" (*Production*, p. 88) which is also closest to identity. The metamorphoses or "transmutations" are themselves principles of invariance, the metaphysical paradigm or hypogram of the "invariant variable." We even return, with greatly increased refinement, to the linearity of reading which was asserted somewhat too literally in the polemics with Roman Jakobson; since the phenomenality of reading is never questioned, its linearity, all appearances to the contrary, is equally safe. "The simultaneous perception of the formal differences and of their semantic equivalents, of a polarity that both opposes and links the textual and the paragrammatic sequence, is precisely what explains the effectiveness of literary discourse. And this is where linearity and non-linearity seem to be reconcilable: the result or effect of the non-linearity of the paragrammization is perceptible only in the anomalies of the lacunae that break the linear sequence" (*Production*, p. 86). The discontinuity, the apparent unreason of nonsensical poetic diction is the best guarantee of the possibility of rational discourse; there is nothing reason seems better able to cope with than its formal negation. In a suggestive *mise en abyme*, Riffaterre describes a text by Francis Ponge in a manner that evokes the scientific detachment of his own tone: Ponge "spurns tradition and proposes instead a praise cleansed of cloying lyricism, in images drawn from the appropriate language, the scientific discourse of crystallography"; the rhetorical "language of flowers" of poetry is told in the hard "language of crystals" of objective cognitive discourse, exactly as Riffaterre shuns the effects of "beautiful" writing by which the commentator fulfills his own pseudo-poetic impulses at the expense of the text on which he comments. He himself writes ironically in the mode of a pedantic philologist. But "since the crystal is a stone indeed but a stone that behaves like a flower, the intertextual conflict is resolved or translated into a reciprocal equivalence, the text's esthetic (lexical) unity is demonstrated, and verbal appropriateness is proven again at the point of maximal departure from cognitive language" (*Semiotics*, p. 114). This "maximal departure" is never further away than day is away from night. It is the alternating and symmetrical plus and minus of knowledge that guarantees the repetition of the same within variance, *das Eine in sich selber unterschiedne, hen diapheron auto*. This pedagogue of literature has the stature of a classical metaphysician, a Platonic swan disguised in the appearance of a technician of teaching: "c'est en saignant que le cygne devient un signe enseignant" (*Production*, p. 81).

Riffaterre, I trust, would rightly not construe anything that has been said as a critique of his theory or of his work. In the ideological climate of the day, which tends to valorize the irrational in many guises and to denounce any attempt to withstand it as philistine timidity, it is tempting to interpret Riffaterre's consistency as merely defensive or evasive. This will not begin to suffice if one is to meet the challenge of his interpretive labors and to counter their persuasive power. It would be all too facile, for example, to point to the psychological implications of Riffaterre's model, in which the mathematical as well as the maternal implications of the "matrix" are obvious, or of his literary examples, with their obsessional stress on death, on sarcophagi, on a not altogether simple sexuality, on hallucination and on obsession itself. If morbidity happens to be one's measure of theoretical audacity, Riffaterre is second to none. The assimilating power of his system is perfectly capable of subsuming the structure of many Freudian insights as it subsumes those of Saussure. The challenge would have to come from authors with a comparable flair for textual reading as well as for the semiosis of the signifier. Riffaterre stakes out his own position in fruitful exchange with structural poetics, of the Slavic as well as of the French variety. Greimas makes few appearances in his footnotes but does not pose a genuine challenge. Bakhtin would be more of a problem, for the reader/text relationship, in Riffaterre, is dialectical rather than dialogical. Even more incompatible with the theory, though only in part with the practice of his reading, would be, of course, Derrida's prudent but trenchant critique of the ontologization of phenomenalism and of formalism as principles of closure. Riffaterre has recently paid Derrida the compliment (as well as practiced on him the legitimate gambit) of treating a text of his as he treats texts of Hugo, Baudelaire or Ponge. This is an unusual occurrence, for philosophical texts are rarely needed as intertexts for his readings; he therefore sensibly avoids the additional problems they inflict upon semiotic and stylistic analyses. The results of his reading of the opening page of *Glas*, in "La trace de l'intertexte,"[13] are revealing for what we can, at long last, identify as Riffaterre's blind spot: his refusal to acknowledge the textual inscription of semantic determinants within a non-determinable system of figuration.

Riffaterre's brief but impeccable reading of the opening three paragraphs of the left column of *Glas* is offered by him as a reconfirmation of his conviction that paragrammatic intertexts are instruments of overdetermination and guarantors, in the final analysis, not only of the possibility but of the imperative coercion of definite readings. When an intertext is only contingently allusive or citational, no genuinely poetic intertextuality is involved; only if a closely intertwined network is produced on the level of the signifier as well as on that of the semiosis are we dealing with truly poetic invention. Riffaterre can then demonstrate with precision and elegance that this is indeed the case in Derrida's text.

In the process, he has, as a matter of course, to encounter the intertext which is written all over *Glas*: the first chapter of Hegel's *Phenomenology of the Spirit* entitled "Sensory Evidence" (*Die sinnliche Gewissheit oder das Diese und das Meinen*) and especially the discussion of the "here" and the "now" that is implied in any determination. Since this text deals with the possible homogeneity between phenomenal and cognitive experience (*wahrnehmen* — perceiving — as *ich nehme wahr* — I acquire in the mode of the true), it has a special significance for Riffaterre, whose own model depends entirely on this possibility. He paraphrases the crux in Hegel's argument as follows: "Hegel . . . has no difficulty showing that *here* and *now* become false and misleading at the moment we write them down" ("Trace," p. 7). This, as the saying goes, is hardly what Hegel said or meant to say, though it is certainly close to what Riffaterre has been saying all along, namely that literary language (language "written down") is capable of referential agrammaticality. One has indeed "pas de peine" in showing that this is the case, but the fact that it took Hegel thousands and thousands of pages to try to circumvent, and yet to confront, the problem would seem to indicate that something else is at stake. At that moment in the *Phenomenology* Hegel is not speaking of language at all, let alone of writing something down, but of consciousness in general as *certainty* in its relation to the phenomenal categories of time, space and selfhood. The point is that this certainty vanishes as soon as any phenomenal determination, temporal or other, is involved, as it always has to be. Consciousness ("here" and "now") is not "false and misleading" because of language; consciousness *is* language, and nothing else, because it is false and misleading. And it is false and misleading because it determines by showing (*montrer* or *démontrer, deiknumi*) or pointing (*Zeigen* or *Aufzeigen*), that is to say in a manner that implies the generality of the phenomenon as cognition (which makes the pointing possible) in the loss of the immediacy and the particularity of sensory perception (which makes the pointing necessary): consciousness is linguistic because it is deictic. Language appears explicitly for the first time in Hegel's chapter in the figure of a *speaking* consciousness: "The assertion (that the reality or the being of external things possess absolute truth for consciousness) does not know what it *states* (*spricht*), does not know that it says (*sagt*) the opposite of what it wants to say (*sagen will*) . . Every consciousness *states* (*spricht*) the opposite of (such a truth)."[14] The figure of a speaking consciousness is made plausible by the deictic function that it names. As for written or inscribed language, it appears in Hegel's text only in the most literal of ways: by means of the parabasis which suddenly confronts us with the actual piece of paper on which Hegel, at that very moment and in this very place, has been writing about the impossibility of ever saying the only thing one wants to say, namely the certainty of sense perception. Particularity (the here and now) was lost long ago, even before speech (*Sprache*): writing this knowledge down in no way loses (nor, of course, recovers) a here and a now that, as Hegel puts it, was never accessible (*erreichbar*) to consciousness or to speech. It does something very different: unlike the here and the now of speech, the here and the now of the inscription is neither false nor misleading: because he wrote it down, the existence of a here and a now of Hegel's text is undeniable as well as totally blank. It reduces, for example, the entire text of the *Phenomenology* to the endlessly repeated stutter: *this* piece of paper, *this* piece of paper, and so on. We can easily enough learn to care for the other examples Hegel mentions: a house, a tree, night, day — but who cares for his darned piece of paper, the last thing in the world we want to hear about and, precisely because it is no longer an *example* but a fact, the only thing we actually get. As we would say, in colloquial exasperation with an obtuse bore: forget it! Which turns out to be precisely what Hegel sees as the function of writing: writing is what prevents speech from taking place, from *zum Worte zu kommen*, from ever reaching the *word* of Saussure's hypogram, and thus to devour itself as the animal is said to devour sensory things (sect. 20, p. 87), in the knowledge that it is false and misleading. Writing is what makes one forget speech: "Natural consciousness therefore proceeds by itself to this outcome, which is its truth, and experiences this progression within itself; but it also always *forgets it* over and again and recommences this movement from the start" (sect. 20, pp. 86-87; italics mine). As the only particular event that can be pointed out, writing, unlike speech and cognition, is what takes us back to this ever-recurring natural consciousness. Hegel, who is often said to have "forgotten" about writing, is unsurpassed in his ability to remember that one should never forget to forget. To write down *this* piece of paper (contrary to saying it) is no longer deictic, no longer a gesture of pointing rightly or wrongly, no longer an example or a *Beispiel*,[15] but the definitive erasure of a forgetting that leaves no trace. It is, in other words, the determined elimination of determination. As such, it goes entirely against the grain of Riffaterre's rational determination of unreason.

At any rate, it makes him misread Hegel (and Derrida) when he summarizes them as stating: "the only *that* (ça) which gives certainty is an abstract *that*, the fact of pointing one's finger, obtained by negating the multitude of *heres* and *nows* that concretize *that*" ("Trace," p. 7). "Pointer du doigt," which is indeed the abstraction par excellence, belongs to language as gesture and as voice, to speech (*Sprache*) and not to writing, which cannot be said, in the last analysis, to point at all. It is consistent with Riffaterre's system that he would have to misinterpret loss of determination as mere loss of reference, but it also marks the limitations of the system. The notion of hypogram allows him to discover the correct intertextual structure of the Derrida passage in the interplay between Derrida, Mallarmé, and Hegel, but it forecloses access to the "donnée sémantique" of a subtext (Hegel) which disposes once and forever of the possibility of determining any such *donnée*. In the case of this particular Riffaterre paper, the system undone is that of the opposition between an aleatory (random) and a necessary intertextual relationship, the opposition which structures the argument. For the patent overdetermination of Derrida's writing, demonstrated beyond any possible doubt, is of poetic significance only if, like Saussure's hypogram, it cannot be determined whether it is random or determined. Overdetermining is a symptom of despair (*Verzweiflung*) as well as of control, and Derrida is not exactly the author who will make it easier to decide between these alternatives.[16]

The stabilization of form and of reading that the model of the hypotext allows is decisively disturbed by these considerations. A correct descriptive observation leads to fallacious hermeneutic conclusions, such as the assurance that Derrida's text is not aleatory or Hegel's text about the suspension of reference. But, in saying this, we have not fulfilled the obligation to supply evidence that certain dimensions of specific texts are beyond the reach of a theoretical model that they put in jeopardy. This obligation persists, for the misconstruction of Hegel or Derrida is not by itself conclusive. It might be, as we observed before, that the practice of reading remains ahead of the theorization and that a further refinement of the model could close the gap.

Riffaterre seems to have reacted to pressures such as these, for the concluding chapter of *Semiotics of Poetry* reveals shifts in tone that cannot be ignored. The ghost of referentiality, which has theoretically been exorcized in the model of the hypogram, does not seem to have been entirely laid to rest. We hear that reading is "at once restrictive and unstable," which is surprising, since the main reason for one's willingness to accept the restrictions was that they had such stabilizing power. We hear that the "revelation" of correct reading "is always chancy, must always begin anew," that "the reader's manufacture of meaning is thus not so much a progress through the poem . . . as it is a seesaw scanning of the text, compelled by the very duality of the signs,'' that reading ''is a continual recommencing, an undecisiveness resolved one moment and lost the next'' (*Semiotics*, pp. 165-66). This language surprises at the conclusion of such an admirably clear and decisive book, a model *text* book in the most laudative sense of the term. It also reveals an anxiety that proves the philosophical vigilance of an author who will not allow method to override truth. It may also be the moment, in Riffaterre, when the theory, instead of lagging behind, has moved ahead of the textual practice.

What would such a practice have to be like in order to correspond to the power of these insights? What, if anything, has Riffaterre omitted from his actual textual readings?

In one of his tentative notes, Saussure discusses the various uses of the word hypogram in Greek. The very sketchy passage is as unclear as it is tantalizing (*Mots*, pp. 30-31 and note 1 on p. 31). Saussure notes and seems to be disturbed by the meaning of *hypographein* as ''signature,'' but he also mentions a ''more special, though more widespread meaning as 'to underscore by means of makeup the features of a face' (*souligner au moyen du fard les traits du visage*)'' (p. 31). This usage is not incompatible with his own adoption of the term which, by analogy, ''underscores a name, a word, by trying to repeat its syllables, and thus giving it another, artificial, mode of being added, so to speak, to the original mode of being of the word.'' *Hypographein* is close in this meaning to *prosopon*, mask or face. Hypogram is close to prosopopeia, the trope of apostrophe. This is indeed compatible with Saussure's use of ''hypogram,'' provided one assumes, once again, the stable existence of an original face that can be embellished, underscored, accentuated or supplemented by the hypogram. But *prosopon-poiein* means to *give* a face and therefore implies that the original face can be missing or nonexistent. The trope which coins a name for a still unnamed entity, which gives face to the faceless is, of course, catachresis. That a catachresis can be a prosopopeia, in the etymological sense of ''giving face,'' is clear from such ordinary instances as the *face* of a mountain or the *eye* of a hurricane. But it is possible that, instead of prosopopeia being a subspecies of the generic type catachresis (or the reverse), the relationship between them is more disruptive than that between genus and species. And what would this imply for the textual model of the hypogram?

Such questions belong to the field of tropology, a part of rhetoric which Riffaterre acknowledges, albeit somewhat grudgingly. As a matter of fact, the very first sentence of the *Essais de stylistique structurale* denounces normative rhetoric as an obstacle to stylistic analysis — something which, in the context of French pedagogy, is certainly to the point. By the time of *Semiotics of Poetry*, after Jakobson, Barthes, and Genette (not to mention Derrida's ''White Mythology''), the term rhetoric has evolved a great deal and can no longer be dismissed so casually. Riffaterre remains consistent, however, in keeping his distance from any suggestion that rhetorical categories might lead a life of their own that is not determined by grammatical structures. At the very onset of *Semiotics of Poetry*, in a rare dogmatic moment, he declares: ''I am aware that many such descriptions [of the structure of meaning in a poem], often founded upon rhetoric, have already been put forward, and I do not deny the usefulness of notions like figure and trope. But whether these categories are well defined . . . or are catchalls . . . they can be arrived at independently of a theory of reading or the concept of text'' (*Semiotics*, p. 1). Since it can be and has been argued that no theory of reading can avoid being a theory of tropes, and since the notion of hypogram, from the start, is intertwined with a specific tropological function (namely catachresis by prosopopeia)[17] Riffaterre's assertion stands or falls with the practical results of the readings it makes possible. Do these readings cope with the sheer strength of figuration, that is to say master their power to confer, to usurp, and to take away significance from grammatical universals? To some extent, the readings confront the interplay between tropes. They have no difficulty incorporating the Jakobsonian pair of metaphor and metonymy within their trans-formational logic;[18] they can account for various catachretic coinages.[19] But how do they confront the trope which threatens to dismember or to disfigure the lexicality and grammaticality of the hypogram, namely prosopopeia which, as the trope of address, is the very figure of the reader and of reading? It is again a sign of Riffaterre's very sound philosophical and rhetorical instincts that, although the figure of prosopopeia is downplayed or even avoided in his terminol-ogy, it reasserts itself as the central trope of the poetic corpus which, more than any other, is the model for the textual system he has so carefully worked out: the corpus of the poetry (and the prose) of Victor Hugo.[20]

For all too obvious reasons of economy, the demonstration of this point will have to be confined to one single instance, the reading of the Hugo poem ''Ecrit sur la vitre d'une fenêtre flamande'' in the paper entitled ''Le poème comme représentation: une lecture de Hugo'' (*Production*, pp. 175-98). The text of the brief poem is as follows:

> *J'aime le carillon dans tes cités antiques,*
> *O vieux pays gardien de tes moeurs domestiques,*
> *Noble Flandre, où le Nord se réchauffe engourdi*
> *Au soleil de Castille et s'accouple au Midi!*
> 5 *Le carillon, c'est l'heure inattendue et folle,*
> *Que l'oeil croit voir, vêtue en danseuse espagnole,*
> *Apparaître soudain par le trou vif et clair*
> *Que ferait en s'ouvrant une porte de l'air.*
> *Elle vient, secouant sur les toits léthargiques*

10 *Son tablier d'argent plein de notes magiques,*
    Réveillant sans pitié les dormeurs ennuyeux,
    Sautant à petits pas comme un oiseau joyeux,
    Vibrant, ainsi qu'un dard qui tremble dans la cible;
    Par un frêle escalier de cristal invisible,
15 *Effarée et dansante, elle descend des cieux;*
    Et l'esprit, ce veilleur fait d'oreilles et d'yeux,
    Tandis qu'elle va, vient, monte et descend encore,
    Entende de marche en marche errer son pied sonore!

Riffaterre analyzes the text as an example of descriptive poetry and uses it to demonstrate that the poetic representation, in the case of such a description, is not based on the reproduction or on the imitation of an external referent, but on the expansion of a hypogram, matrix or cliché that functions in a purely verbal way: "It is not the external reality that is poetic but the manner in which it is described and in which it is 'seen' from the point of view of the words (*à partir des mots*)" (*Production*, p. 178) or, even more forcefully: "Literary description only apparently returns us to things, to signifieds; in fact, poetic representation is founded on a reference to the signifiers" (*Production*, p. 198). This not only allows him to avoid the usual platitudes about Hugo's travels and tastes but it also allows him to account for several of the details that organize the text and that have indeed little to do with the perceptual outline of the entity that is being described. It allows him, finally, to account for the *rightness* of the figural vehicles that were chosen, not in terms of the accuracy of actual observation (bound to be endless in its denotations and therefore always arbitrary and inconclusive) but in terms of the interplay between several verbal systems that restrict and define each other by mutual convergence or contrast. The representation of the clock as a Spanish dancer as well as a bird, of the chimed tune as an ascending and descending staircase as well as an overspilling apron, and several other apparently incompatible details, are shown to be generated by a common matrix. This matrix generates, by way of a set of clichés, its own system of hypograms. This "donnée sémantique" is identified as "carillon flamand," which produces by amplification the determining configurations of descriptive systems that make up the poem. One will find little room for disagreement in any of Riffaterre's descriptions of the description which the poem is supposed to perform.

The descriptive system "carillon flamand" can indeed be said to occur in the poem but it begins only by line 5 and the three concluding lines are not, strictly speaking, a part of it. It is in fact not in the least certain that the poem is descriptive at all: a title such as "Le carillon," which would perhaps be suitable for Rilke's *New Poem* on the same topic, "Quai du rosaire," would not be fitting. The "description," if description there is, is embedded within a very different frame. The poem is a declaration of love addressed to something or someone, staged as an address of one subject to another in a *je-tu* situation which can hardly be called descriptive.

> *J'aime le carillon dans tes cités antiques*
> *O vieux pays gardien de tes moeurs domestiques. . .*

The apostrophe, the address (*O vieux pays* . . .), frames the description it makes possible. It is indeed a prosopopeia, a giving face to two entities, "l'heure" and "l'esprit," which are most certainly deprived of any literal face. Yet by the end of the poem, it is possible to identify without fail the *je* and the *tu* of line 1 as being time and mind. The figuration occurs by ways of this address. Riffaterre notes this — it would indeed be difficult to overlook it — but does not seem to consider it as being in any way remarkable, stylistically or otherwise. He calls it personification and dismisses it from his commentary by stressing the banality of "describing, once again, a reality in terms of another, the inanimate by ways of the animated" (*Production*, p. 177). Now it is certainly beyond question that the figure of address is recurrent in lyric poetry, to the point of constituting the generic definition of, at the very least, the ode (which can, in its turn, be seen as paradigmatic for poetry in general). And that it therefore occurs, like all figures, in the guise of a cliché or a convention is equally certain. None of this would allow one to discard or to ignore it as the main generative force that produces the poem in its entirety. For the singularity of "Ecrit sur la vitre d'une fenêtre flamande" does not primarily consist of the surprising details; these "descriptions" can only occur because a consciousness or a mind (*l'esprit*) is figurally said to relate to another abstraction (time) as male relates to female in a copulating couple (line 5). The matrix, in other words, is not "carillon" but "j'aime le carillon," and this matrix is not a "donnée sémantique" but is itself already a figure: it is not supposed to describe some peculiar sexual perversion, such as chronophilia, since the persons involved in this affair are persons only by dint of linguistic figuration. The description that follows, one single sentence extending over 13 lines, is a mere expansion, in Riffaterre's sense of the term, of the original figure. It does not describe an entity, referential or textual, but sets up a rapport between concepts said to be structured like a sense perception: the sentence culminates in the verb *to hear* ("Le carillon, c'est l'heure . . . Et l'esprit (*l*)'*entend*" which carries the full burden of dramatic resolution and intelligibility. As in Hegel's first chapter of the *Phenomenology*, the figural enigma is that of a conscious cognition being, in some manner, akin to the certainty of a sense perception. This may be a classical philosopheme, but not a kernel of determined meaning.

Riffaterre is certainly right in saying that what is presumably being described is not referential but verbal. The verbal entity, or function, is not, however, the signifier "carillon" but the figure *l'esprit entend* (as well as "voit" and, eventually, "aime") *le temps*.[21] The text is therefore not the mimesis of a signifier but of a specific figure, prosopopeia. And since mimesis is itself a figure, it is the figure of a figure (the prosopopeia of a prosopopeia) and not in any respect, neither in appearance nor in reality, a description — as little as the alliterating bottles or the synecdochal churches in Proust's *Recherche* are descriptions. A proper title for Hugo's poem could be "Prosopopée" rather than "Le carillon," not just in the vague and general manner in which any poem of address could be given this title,[22] but in the very specific way that the burden of understanding and of persuasion, in this poem, corresponds exactly to the epistemological tension that produces prosopopeia, the master trope of poetic discourse. The actual title, however, is "Ecrit sur la vitre d'une fenêtre flamande," the "here" and the "now" of the poem which elicits no comment from Riffaterre and remains to be accounted for.

The relationship between the carillon and time should be of special interest to a semiotician, for it is analogous to the relationship between signifier and signified that constitutes the sign. The ringing of the bells (or the conventional tune that serves as the prelude to the actual chimes) is the material sign of an event (the passage of time) of which the phenomenality lacks certainty; just as it has been said that, if it were not for novels, no one would know for certain that he is in love, in the absence of chimes and clocks no one could be certain that such a thing as time exists, in the full ontological sense of that term. For as most philosophers well know, the very concept of certainty, which is the basis of all concepts, comes into being only in relation to sensory experience be it, as in Hegel, as unmediated assurance or, as in Descartes, as reflected delusion. If there is to be consciousness (or experience, mind, subject, discourse, or face), it has to be susceptible of phenomenalization. But since the phenomenality of experience cannot be established *a priori*, it can only occur by a process of signification. The phenomenal and sensory properties of the signifier have to serve as guarantors for the certain existence of the signified and, ultimately, of the referent. The carillon's relationship to time has to be like the relationship of the mind to the senses: it is the sonorous face, the "masque aux yeux sonores" (Rilke) of cognition which, by metonymic substitution, links the sound of the bells to the face of the clock. Once the phenomenal intuition has been put in motion, all other substitutions follow as in a chain. But the starting, catachretic decree of signification is arbitrary. This text, like all texts, has to adhere to the program of these problematics, regardless of the philosophical knowledge or skill of its author. It accomplishes the trick by arbitrarily linking the mind to the semiotic relationship that connects the bells to the temporal motion they signify. The senses become the signs of the mind as the sound of the bells is the sign of time, because time and mind are linked, in the figure, as in the embrace of a couple. This declaration ("'j'aime le carillon" or *l'esprit aime le temps*) is then acted out, in the erotic mode of "mere" sense perception,[23] in the allegory of cognition that follows, a seduction scene that culminates in the extraordinary line, the prosopopeia of prosopopeia:

> *Et l'esprit, ce veilleur fait d'oreilles et d'yeux* . . .

This bizarre waking monster, made of eyes and ears as mud is made of earth and water, is so eminently visible that any attentive reader will have to respond to it. It is the visual shape of something that has no sensory existence: a hallucination. As any reader of Hugo or, for that matter, anyone who ever wondered about the *legs* of a table or, like Wordsworth, about the *faces* or the *backs* of mountains, knows, prosopopeia is hallucinatory. To make the invisible visible is uncanny. A reader of Riffaterre's caliber can be counted on to respond in this fashion. One of his earliest essays, going back almost twenty years, collected in the *Essais de stylistique structurale* is entitled "La vision hallucinatoire chez Victor Hugo." The tone and the technique may appear quite "ideological," especially if compared to the later rigor, but the essay already struggles valiantly to keep literary effects and psychological experience apart. The analysis is stylistic in name only, since Riffaterre still uses thematic procedures which critics like Poulet or Bachelard had been using for non-stylistic aims. But the programmatic aim is clearly stated: what the poems give us is not a hallucination but a hallucinatory effect. The same clear distinction is stated in a footnote to the crucial word *invisible* in our present poem: " 'veilleur fait d'oreilles et d'yeux' sharply distinguishes between two orders of sensation . . . the transposition from the auditive to the visual is therefore not represented as a synesthesia, but as hallucination. Hallucination is poetically effective, but from the viewpoint of poetic mimesis, it is still an excuse, the avowal of a necessary reference to a rational context" (*Production*, p. 186, note 1). Once again, what should give one pause in statements such as these is not the assertion of non-referentiality, which is obvious, but the implied assertion of semantic determination of which non-referentiality is the specular negation. Descartes found it difficult to distinguish between waking and sleeping because, when one dreams, one always dreams that one is awake, just as Hugo's "mind" is awake (*l'esprit, ce veilleur* . . .). How then is one to decide on the distinction between hallucination and perception since, in hallucination, the difference between *I see* and *I think that I see* has been one-sidedly resolved in the direction of apperception? Consciousness has become consciousness only of itself. In that sense, any consciousness, including perception, is hallucinatory: one never "has" a hallucination the way one has a sore foot from kicking the proverbial stone. Just as the hypothesis of dreaming undoes the certainty of sleep, the hypothesis, or the figure, of hallucination undoes sense certainty. This means, in linguistic terms, that it is impossible to say whether

prosopopeia is plausible because of the empirical existence of dreams and hallucinations or whether one believes that such a thing as dreams and hallucinations
exists because language permits the figure of prosopopeia. The question "Was
it a vision or a waking dream?" is destined to remain unanswered. Prosopopeia
undoes the distinction between reference and signification on which all semiotic
systems, including Riffaterre's, depend.

The claim of all poetry to make the invisible visible is a figure to the precise
extent that it undoes the distinction between sign and trope. It smuggles the
wiles of rhetoric back into the hygienic clarity of semiotics. This claim is overtly
stated in Hugo's poem, and it puts a particularly heavy burden on the word
"invisible" that appears in the text (line 14). Riffaterre comments on the line

Par un frêle escalier de cristal invisible
. . . elle [l'heure] descend des cieux

by stressing (1) the hyperbolic function of the tautology "cristal invisible"
which makes the crystal even more crystalline and (2) the negative power of the
epithet which replaces the architectural, spatial, and hence visible, staircase by
an invisible one. It thus prepares the transfer from sight to sound in the concluding
line. In the descriptive context to which Riffaterre has chosen to confine himself,
the two observations, as well as their combined overdetermining effect, are
entirely correct. These descriptive strategies of intra-sensory circulations are
inscribed however within a wider scene, in which the interaction does not occur
between one kind of sense experience and another but between, on the one side,
the sensory as such and, on the other, the non-sensory mind. This is why, in
the line "l'esprit, ce veilleur fait d'oreilles et d'yeux," as Riffaterre correctly
observes, eyes and ears are treated as separate but equal, without dialectical
tension between them. What in Baudelaire's "Correspondances" is achieved by
infinite expansion, the confusion and unification of the various sensory faculties,
is here achieved by the figure of the initial apostrophe;[24] therefore, it is the
authority of that figure, and not of a synecdoche of totalization that does not
appear in the poem, that has to be examined. Aside from the functions pointed
out by Riffaterre, "cristal invisible" functions in still another register which
carries, for the poem as a whole, the burden of a heavier investment. By way
of the mediation of the scaled stairways time can be called an invisible *cristal*;
the materiality of crystal, which is at least accessible to one of the senses, can
serve the insistent strategy of the poem in helping to make the elusive passage
of time accessible to sight and sound. But there is another "cristal" in the poem
which is no longer invisible and which also achieves materiality, albeit in a very
different manner: namely the window on which, according to the title, the poem
is supposed to have been written. Because the poem is written on the transparent
window, the window has indeed become visible and one could consider this

metamorphosis as one more figure for the linkage between mind and senses. By coining the prosopopeia of address, Hugo has time and mind reflect each other in a couple as inseparable as Narcissus's eye is inseparable from his reflected face. But that is not all there is to the title. Unlike everything else in the poem, the title contains an element that is not hallucinatory. Every detail as well as every general proposition in the text is fantastic except for the assertion, in the title, that it is *écrit*, written. That it was supposed to be written, like Swift's love poem to Stella, as words upon a window pane, is one more cliché to add to those Riffaterre has already collected. But that, like Hegel's text from the *Phenomenology*, it was written cannot be denied. The materiality (as distinct from the phenomenality) that is thus revealed, the unseen "cristal" whose existence thus becomes a certain *there* and a certain *then* which can become a *here* and a *now* in the reading "now" taking place, is not the materiality of the mind or of time or of the carillon — none of which exist, except in the figure of prosopopeia — but the materiality of an inscription. Description, it appears, was a device to conceal inscription. Inscription is neither a figure, nor a sign, nor a cognition, nor a desire, nor a hypogram, nor a matrix, yet no theory of reading or of poetry can achieve consistency if, like Riffaterre's, it responds to its powers only by a figural evasion which, in this case, takes the subtly effective form of evading the figural.

Notes

1. See, for example, as one instance among many, Descartes' discussion of teaching in "Réponses aux secondes objections [contre les *Méditations*]," in *Oeuvres philosophiques*, ed. Fernand Alquié (Paris: Garnier, 1967), II, 583ff.

2. *Semiotics of Poetry* (Bloomington: Indiana University Press, 1978), p. 115; *La production du texte* (Paris: Seuil, 1979), p. 7, available as *Text Production*, trans. Terese Lyons (NY: Columbia University Press, 1983). Hereafter *Semiotics* and *Production*. Translations from the latter are my own.

3. See, for example, the critique of a remark by Roland Barthes on a text by Tacitus in *Essais de stylistique structurale*, pp. 281-85. Translations from this book are my own.

4. As distinguished from "meaning" which is referential and not formally encoded.

5. This is also the point of convergence between Riffaterre and the aesthetics of reception of the Konstanz group. The concept of "concretization" in Felix Vodička, which is important for H. R. Jauss and his associates, is close to that of actualization in Riffaterre.

6. One thinks of such widely scattered examples as Proust's critical essays on Balzac and Flaubert or some passages in Sartre's early essays in *Situations I*.

7. Derrida and Foucault are deliberately, and wisely, set apart, since their work does not fit the more strictly technical format of the discussion.

8. In 1971, Jean Starobinski published the much awaited *Les mots sous les mots: les anagrammes de Ferdinand de Saussure* (hereafter *Mots*), followed by further unpublished texts from Saussure's notebooks. It attracted a great deal of attention from various quarters, especially from Julia Kristeva and the *Tel Quel* group. Probably the best account available in English of the theoretical challenge that emanates from these texts is that of Sylvère Lotringer in his essay "The Game of the Name" in *Diacritics* (Summer, 1973), pp. 8-16.

9. On this entire matter, Saussure is particularly troubled, as well as vertiginously speculative,

when he abandons the field of classical Latin poetry and risks some considerations on the Indo-European roots of High-German and Nordic alliterative poetry. See, for example, the section on the German *Stab* (staff) and *Buchstabe* (letter), *Mots*, pp. 38-40.

10. With the sole exception, as far as I know, of a preliminary text, *Anagrammes*, published by Starobinski in *Mercure de France* (February, 1964), to which Derrida refers. The somewhat cryptic existence of Saussure's *cahiers* was a titillating piece of intellectual gossip until the publication of *Les mots sous les mots*.

11. Especially "Paragramme et signifiance" in *Production*; also *Semiotics*, p. 12 and note 16 (p. 168), p. 19 and dispersed throughout the book. Riffaterre's terminology, perhaps in deliberate allusion to Saussure, is not entirely consistent and it is not always easy to separate his use of hypogram, paragram, or even matrix rigorously from each other. It would appear that paragram describes the process of displacement of the hypogram, through an intertext, but it is correct to assume that, since the text is constituted by this very displacement, it would not be crucial to distinguish between hypogram and paragram. The terminological ambivalence is, therefore, to a point, legitimate or unimportant. As for the matrix, the semantic ground of the hypogram prior to a specific lexicalization, it is indeed distinct: the matrix, unlike the hypo- or the paragram, may not be actualized in the text. Riffaterre at times even asserts that it is never actualized but he does not hold to this as a necessary condition in all his examples. My own preference for hypogram has to do with etymological considerations in Saussure that will become apparent later.

12. This allows Riffaterre to claim that he avoids the metaphysical quandary of an originary *locus princeps*, which, as Lotringer shows, underlies Saussure's system by means of the principle of the name.

13. *La Pensée* 215 (October, 1980). Hereafter "Trace."

14. *Phänomenologie des Geistes*, ed. J. Hoffmeister (Hamburg: Felix Meiner, 1952), sect. 20, p. 87. Translation and italics are my own.

15. On *Beispiel* in Chapter 1 of the *Phenomenology*, see Andrzej Warminski, "Reading for Example: 'Sense Certainty' in Hegel's *Phenomenology of Spirit* in *Diacritics* (Summer, 1981), pp.83-94.

16. The divergence between Riffaterre and Derrida becomes at once apparent in the next paragraph of *Glas* which has to do, among other things, with the possibility of teaching: "Perhaps there is an incompatibility, rather than a dialectical contradiction, between teaching and the act of signing, a magister and a signatary."

17. See Saussure's comparable hesitation about the relationship between hypogram and trope: in his case, the trope under consideration is that of paranomasia (*Mots*, p. 32).

18. There are numerous examples throughout the work of the metonymisation of apparently metaphorical structures, a technique of rhetorical analysis that Riffaterre shares with Gérard Genette. For one particularly striking instance, see *Semiotics*, p. 122 (on *ardoise* in Ponge).

19. See, for instance, "Poétique du néologisme," Chapter IV of *Production*, or the observations on a poem by Queneau in *Semiotics*.

20. The *Essais de stylistique structurale* could be said, without exaggeration, to be a book on Victor Hugo: the essays were originally destined, I believe, to be just that. *Semiotics of Poetry* deals primarily with symbolist and surrealist poets in the wake of Hugo. There is, of course, historical justification for this grouping, for the impact of Hugo on French nineteenth- and twentieth-century poetry is comparable only to that of Goethe on German poetry of the same period, or of Milton and Spenser combined on English Romanticism. If so-called symbolist and surrealist French poetry has a "face," it is that of Hugo.

21. See Riffaterre's justification of the use of verbs of perception (*Production*, p. 191). The point is not how fictive persons ("des personnages") are being affected by time since what is here being affected are not persons, real or fictional, but mind, in the most general sense conceivable.

22. As they in fact often are, though preferably by the more euphonic and noble term "ode" or "Ode to X."

23. Rather than being a heightened version of sense experience, the erotic is a figure that makes such experience possible. We do not see what we love but we love in the hope of confirming the illusion that we are indeed seeing anything at all.

24. This simplifies "Correspondances" in a manner that cannot be discussed here. The reference is to the canonical *ideé reçue* of the poem, not to the poem read. [Cf. my "Anthropomorphism and Trope in the Lyric," in *The Rhetoric of Romanticism*, pp. 239-62.]

Reading and History

By his own volition, the work of the German literary historian and theorist Hans Robert Jauss has been associated with a study group for which he is a spokesman and which practices a specific way of investigating and teaching literature. In the field of literary theory, the existence of such groups is not an unusual occurrence. They are, at times, centered on a single, dominating personality and take on all the exalted exclusiveness of a secret society, with its rituals of initiation, exclusion, and hero-worship. Nothing could be more remote from the spirit of the group of which Jauss is a prominent member. The Konstanz school of literary studies, so named because several of its members taught or are teaching at the newly founded University of Konstanz in Southern Germany, is a liberal association of scholars, informally united by methodological concerns that allow for considerable diversity. It has the character of a continuing research seminar that includes some constant members (of which H. R. Jauss is one) next to more casual participants; a somewhat comparable instance of such a group, in structure if not in content, would have been, in this country, the Chicago critics of the forties and fifties, who shared an interest in Aristotelian poetics. The concerns of such groups are methodological rather than, as in the case of the New Criticism or the Frankfurt School, cultural and ideological; their influence is didactic and "scientific" rather than critical. One has to bear this aspect of Jauss's work in mind in reading the essays included in this volume.[1] It accounts for their programmatic and relatively impersonal tone. Whereas the "masters" of an earlier generation in Germany and elsewhere, literary scholars such as Vossler, Spitzer, Curtius, Auerbach, or even Lukács, wrote as individual talents engaged in speculations of their own, Jauss sees himself as a participant on a team that also is concerned with the professional aspects of literary instruction. The attitude is typical for a generation whose approach to literature has become more systematic; it is by no means incompatible with genuine innovation or with wider humanistic commitments. In reading Jauss, one is not reading the work of a speculative philosopher, a literary critic, or a pure theoretician of poetics. One is, first of all, reading the work of a specialist of French literature who has made contributions to a remarkably diverse number of topics, from medieval genre theory to Marcel Proust.[2] But, beyond this, one is also reading the work of a theoretically informed, learned, and enlightened expert whose work fully warrants extended theoretical discussion and didactic application.

The methodology of the Konstanz school is mostly referred to as *Rezeptionsästhetik*, a word that does not lend itself easily to translation into English. We speak in this country of reader-response criticism or, more imaginatively (though also more controversially), of "affective stylistics."[3] These terms stress reading as a constitutive element of any text but, except for the implicit connotations of "stylistic" or "poetics," they put less emphasis on the far-reaching, traditional word "aesthetics" that remains of central importance to Jauss and his associates. What has to be called, somewhat awkwardly, the "aesthetics of reception" has itself been well received in this country. It has been a two-way process; the University of Konstanz may be as far removed from a large urban center as is possible in today's Germany, but there is nothing provincial about the Konstanz school. From the start, in 1963, the colloquia of the group included participants from the United States and a recent anthology of their main position papers includes contributions from Michael Riffaterre and Stanley Fish.[4] Conversely, leading members of the Konstanz group such as Wolfgang Iser, Jurij Striedter, and Hans Robert Jauss himself often teach in this country, some on a permanent basis. Leading American journals publish and review their papers; the books of Wolfgang Iser, whose field is English literature, have been translated and are being extensively used and debated by American specialists of narrative fiction. With the publication of Jauss's *Toward an Aesthetic of Reception* the introduction of the Konstanz school to American readers is made complete. It makes available some of the most lucidly argued theoretical documents to have originated in the group. They are indeed so clear and convincing as to require little introduction. Since they are rooted, however, in a methodological and philosophical tradition only remotely comparable to our own, it may be useful to see how Jauss's presuppositions are revealed and put into perspective by approaches that developed in different circumstances.

The aim of the Konstanz theoreticians can be derived from the general title given to their main publication series: Poetics *and* Hermeneutics.[5] The *and* that appears in this combination is not as obvious as it might seem. Hermeneutics is, by definition, a process directed toward the determination of meaning; it postulates a transcendental function of understanding, no matter how complex, deferred, or tenuous it might be, and will, in however mediated a way, have to raise questions about the extralinguistic truth value of literary texts. Poetics, on the other hand, is a metalinguistic, descriptive or prescriptive discipline that lays claim to scientific consistency. It pertains to the formal analysis of linguistic entities as such, independently of signification; as a branch of linguistics, it deals with theoretical models prior to their historical realization. Hermeneutics belongs traditionally to the sphere of theology and to its secular prolongation in the various historical disciplines; unlike poetics, which is concerned with the taxonomy and the interaction of poetic structures, hermeneutics is concerned with the meaning of specific texts. In a hermeneutic enterprise, reading necessarily intervenes but, like computation in algebraic proof, it is a means toward an end, a means that should finally become transparent and superfluous; the ultimate aim of a hermeneutically successful reading is to do away with reading altogether.[6] It is not easy to say how reading is involved, if at all, in poetics. If — to abuse once more one of the most outworn examples in literature — on noting that Homer refers to Achilles as a lion, I conclude that Achilles is courageous, this is a hermeneutic decision; if, on the other hand, I examine, with Aristotle, whether Homer is using a simile or a metaphor,[7] this is a consideration in the sphere of poetics. The two procedures have very little in common. It is clear, however, from this loaded example (loaded because, by selecting a figure of speech, one has in fact pre-emptied the question) that one has to have "read" the text in terms of poetics to arrive at a hermeneutic conclusion. One has to have become aware that it is a figure, otherwise one would simply take it to mean that Achilles has changed species or that Homer has taken leave of his senses. But one also has to read it hermeneutically to "understand" it as poetics: one has to ac-knowledge Achilles' courage as well as his humanity to notice that something occurs in the language that does not normally occur in the natural or social world, that a lion can be substituted for a man. All that this hasty piece of improvised poetics is meant to suggest is that hermeneutics and poetics, different and distinct as they are, have a way of becoming entangled, as indeed they have since Aristotle and before. One can look upon the history of literary theory as the continued attempt to disentangle this knot and to record the reasons for failing to do so.

The boldness of the Konstanz school in calling their approach a poetics as well as a hermeneutics measures the scope and the burden of its contribution. In practice, the distribution of competencies as well as the rather complex methodological genealogy of the group has divided the emphasis among its various members. Some go back to the structural analyses of the Prague linguistic circle and find their ancestry among the more technical aspects of phenomenology, including the work of the Polish philosopher Roman Ingarden. In their case, the primary emphasis falls on poetics (*Werkstruktur*) rather than on hermeneutics

(*Interpretationssystem*).[8] Others find their antecedents among philosophers of history and interpretation rather than in the structural analysis of language and of consciousness; their primary emphasis is on hermeneutics. The synthesis, the articulation of poetics with hermeneutics remains the common aim of all aestheticians of reception, but the attempted solutions as well as the techniques of reading that lead to these solutions vary, depending on the starting position. If, mostly for the sake of convenience, one chooses to divide the group into poeticians and hermeneuts, then Hans Robert Jauss undoubtedly belongs among the latter. This may give him the appearance of being more traditional, or at least more concerned with tradition, than some of his associates, yet it makes his approach particularly instructive for American readers whose legitimate impatience with the technicalities of formal analysis sends them in search of models for historical understanding.

Jauss's relationship to the hermeneutic tradition is itself by no means simple or uncritical. He fully shares in the stance that unites all members of the group in their common rejection of the "essentialist" conception of literary art. The suspicion of essentialism arises whenever the study of the production or of the structure of literary texts is pursued at the expense of their reception, at the expense of the individual or collective patterns of understanding that issue from their reading and evolve in time. In "Literary History as a Challenge to Literary Theory," the closest Jauss came to writing an actual manifesto, the polemical thrust of the passages in which he sets his methods apart from those of his predecessors allows one to situate this new pragmatism, or this new materialism, within the tradition of German scholarship. Jauss differentiates himself sharply from both the formalistic and the Marxist tendencies that were prevalent at the time. The grounds for his critical attitude toward Marxism (or, to be more precise, toward a certain type of social realism) as well as toward form, turn out to be remarkably similar. Georg Lukács, an avowed Marxist, is criticized for reasons that differ little from those invoked with regard to the anything but Marxist Ernst Robert Curtius. For all their ideological differences, both adhere to the classical creed of the canonical work as the aesthetic incarnation of a universal essence. Curtius's canon, which is that of the masterpieces of the Western neo-Latin tradition, differs entirely from Lukács's, which is that of nineteenth-century realism as it culminates in Balzac and dissolves with Flaubert. But the disagreements between various canons are less important to Jauss than the canonical conception itself, in which the work is assumed to transcend history because it encompasses the totality of its tensions within itself. Lukács and Curtius both remain faithful to such a conception. Even Hans-Georg Gadamer, Jauss's teacher at Heidelberg, whom he has consistently acknowledged as a determining influence, is being reproached for his commitment to the canonical idea of tradition, which in Germany often tends to coincide with the canonization of the Age of Goethe. Jauss's work is part of a reaction against an orthodoxy, an orthodoxy that refuses to admit, as Hegel is supposed to have stated in his *Aesthetics*, that the end of classicism is also the end of art. Hence his continued concern with modernity as the crux of literary history. The question remains to be considered whether Jauss's own historical procedure can indeed claim to free itself from the coercion of a model that is perhaps more powerful, and for less controllable reasons, than its assumed opponents believe.

The strength of Jauss's method stems from a refinement of the established rules for the historical understanding of literature. His interest is no longer directed toward the definition of an actual canon but toward the dynamic and dialectical process of canon formation — a notion that is familiar, in this country, to readers of T. S. Eliot and, more recently and in a very different mode, of Harold Bloom.[9] Such a critique of historical positivism coupled with a critique of essentialism is not in itself new; few historians still believe that a work of the past can be understood by reconstructing, on the basis of recorded evidence, the set of conventions, expectations, and beliefs that existed at the time of its elaboration. What is different and effective in the approach suggested by Jauss are the reasons (implicitly) given for this impossibility: the historical conscious-ness of a given period can never exist as a set of openly stated or recorded propositions. It exists instead, in Jauss's terminology, as a "horizon of expecta-tion." The term, which derives from Husserl's phenomenology of perception in its application to the experience of consciousness, implies that the condition of existence of a consciousness is not available to this consciousness in a conscious mode, just as, in a perception, conscious attention is possible only upon a background, or horizon, of distraction.[10] Similarly, the "horizon of expectation" brought to a work of art is never available in objective or even objectifiable form, neither to its author nor to its contemporaries or later recipients.

This complicates, but also enriches, the process of historical description to a considerable degree. A dialectic of understanding, as a complex interplay between knowing and not-knowing, is built into the very process of literary history. The situation is comparable to the dialogic relationship that develops between the analyst and his interlocutor in psychoanalysis. Neither of the two knows the experience being discussed; they may indeed not even know whether such an experience ever existed. The subject is separated from it by mechanisms of repression, defense, displacement and the like, whereas, to the analyst, it is available only as a dubiously evasive symptom. But this difficulty does not prevent a dialogical discourse of at least some interpretative value from taking place. The two "horizons," that of individual experience and that of methodical understanding, can engage each other and they will undergo modifications in the process, though none of the experiences may ever become fully explicit.

The analogy with psychoanalysis (which Jauss does not use) underscores the epistemological complexity of the historian's task. Both analyst and historian point to a cognition that, for reasons variously identified as psychological, epistemological, or, in the case of Heidegger, ontological, is not available as an actual presence and therefore requires a labor of interpretation or of reading prior even to determining whether it can ever be reached. We have come to expect this degree of hermeneutic intricacy from any philosophical or psychological analysis but, surprisingly enough, a similar subtlety is rarely demanded from historians and, among historians, least of all from literary historians — although, according to the logic of the situation with its implied stress on reading rather than knowing, literary history, rather than psychoanalysis or epistemology, should be the privileged example, the model case. This surprise is in fact not surprising at all, since the reluctance is itself the symptom of an anxiety of not-knowing that may reach further than pragmatic historians may wish to know. Be this as it may, in Jauss's defense of a history and an aesthetics of reception, the model for the historical understanding of literature finally comes of age, as it were, by ways of the negative implications contained in the term "horizon of expectation." His critical descriptions of earlier literary histories draw their energy from this insight and, with few exceptions, these descriptions will be found hard to refute. Jauss's critique of the preconscious or unconscious[11] assumptions that underlie canonical literary history constitutes a major contribution, all the more relevant for us since the same problem exists in this country in a less thematized, more diffused, and therefore all the more coercive way.

The same point of departure, the duplicitous epistemology of the historical consciousness, allows Jauss to defend a far-reaching synthesis between the private and the public dimensions of the literary work. This synthesis constitutes the programmatic and forward-looking, as opposed to the critical, aspects of his work. Thus the passage from the individual to the collective or the social aspects of the work is implicit in the model of the "horizon": just as the anonymous background of a perception is general and undifferentiated with regard to the individual perception that stands foregrounded and silhouetted[12] against it, the particular work, at the moment of its production, stands out in its singularity from the collective grayness of received ideas and ideologies. Preconscious or subconscious expectations are always collective and therefore, to a degree, "received." They are the outcome of a reception by means of which the individual work becomes part of a landscape against which new works will, in turn, be silhouetted. Translated from spatial metaphors into epistemological categories, the process can be stated in terms of question and answer: the question occurs as an individual disruption of an answer that has become common knowledge but which, under the effect of this new question, can now be seen to have itself been an individual response to an earlier, collective question. As the answer metamorphoses into a question, it becomes like an individual, tree, or portrait set within a stylized landscape and it reveals, by the same token, a live background behind its background, in the form of a question from which it now can itself *stand out*. The question-and-answer structure, like the foreground-background or the conscious-preconscious structures, are abyssal frames that engender each other without end or *telos*. In the process, however, they create a sequence of apparent syntheses that convey an impression of methodological mastery. Jauss can legitimately claim that the "horizon of expectation" mediates between the private inception and the public reception of the work. And he can also claim that it mediates between the self-enclosed structure and its outside effect or *Wirkung*. To the extent that the background is collective or "common," it is, at first, nondifferentiated and unstructured; under the impact of the individually structured questions, as understood and identified by the historian-interpreter, it becomes aware of itself as background and acquires, in its turn, the coherence necessary for its organization and potential transformation. Jauss provides a clear example of this process: Emma Bovary, a character in a fictional construct, whose mind is like an amorphous bundle of aberrations against which the beauty of her shape stands silhouetted, engenders, in the mind of her readers, a critical awareness of social conventions strong enough to put these conventions in question. The historical reading as reception mediates between the formal structure and social change.

In the final analysis, the procedure provides a model for the articulation between structure and interpretation. At the moment of its inception, the individual work of art stands out as unintelligible with regard to the prevailing conventions. The only relation it has to them is that of contemporaneity or of synchrony, an entirely contingent and syntagmatic relationship between two elements that happen to coincide in time but are otherwise entirely alien to each other. The differentiation that separates the work from its setting is then inscribed in the historical, diachronic motion of its understanding (*Horizontswandel*), which ends in the discovery of properties held in common between the work and its projected history. Unlike the relationship between the work and its historical present, the relationship between the work and its future is not purely arbitrary. It contains elements of genuine paradigmatic similarity that can circulate freely between the formal singularity of the work and the history of its reception. Put in somewhat more technical terms, one would say that, in Jauss's historical model, a syntagmatic displacement within a synchronic structure becomes, in its reception, a paradigmatic condensation within a diachrony. Attributes of difference and of similarity can be exchanged thanks to the intervention of temporal categories: by allowing the work to exist in time without complete loss of identity, the alienation of its formal structure is suspended by the history of its understanding. Chiasmic patterns of this type never fail to carry the promise of totalization.

One sees that the methodological rewards for the willingness to give up the illusion of unmediated understanding are considerable. Nor are they purely theoretical: Jauss is entirely willing to submit his hermeneutic model to the concrete test of practical interpretation and to refine it in the process. The lack of compatibility between literary theory and practice that plagues the study of literature everywhere thus also seems to be on the way to being overcome by a judicious aesthetics of reception. The persuasiveness of the argument, the validity of the critique of traditional canonical literary history, the considerable contributions to the interpretation of particular texts combine to bear witness to the merits of a method whose influence on the theory and the pedagogy of literary studies has been entirely beneficial. It is an impressive record. If one wishes, in the true spirit of the method, to question in turn the horizon of expectation of the aesthetics of reception, then one should begin by acknowledging the merits of a theory that enables one to ask such a question within a productive context.

Some writers, not very remote from Jauss in time and place, have denied the efficacy of a theory of interpretation based on the public reception of a work of literature and have discarded it as a mere side-effect devoid of hermeneutic interest. Walter Benjamin's dogmatic pronouncement at the onset of his essay entitled "The Task of the Translator" is a relevant case in point: "Nowhere does a concern for the reception of a work of art or of an art form aver itself fruitful for its understanding. . . . No poem is addressed to a reader, no painting to its beholder, no symphony to its listeners."[13] The passage is quoted by Rainer Warning, together with a passage from Adorno, as a prime example of author- or production-oriented essentialism.[14] But is this really the case? When Jauss identifies the power of canonical essences in the writings of Curtius, Lukács, and Gadamer, he is on safe ground, but when the same is being said about Benjamin, Adorno, and Heidegger — three names that, for all that separates them, belong together in this context — things are not so simple. Benjamin, for instance, in the very essay from which the just-quoted passage is taken, could not be more explicit in his critique of Platonic essences as a model for history when he rejects the validity of the notion of copy or representation (*Abbild*) as an approach to literary texts. Nor could one be more eloquently explicit than he is, in the same essay, about the historicity of literary understanding — although the notion of history that Benjamin here invokes certainly differs considerably from Jauss's. By invoking the "translation" rather than the reception or even the reading of a work as the proper analogon for its understanding, the negativity inherent in the process is being recognized: we all know that translations can never succeed and that the task (*Aufgabe*) of the translator also means, as in the parlance of competitive sports, his having to give up, his defeat "by default." But "translation" also directs, by implication, the attention to language, rather than perception, as the possible locus for this negative moment. For translation is, by definition, intralinguistic, not a relationship between a subject and an object, or a foreground and a background, but between one linguistic function and another. Throughout the essay, Benjamin's point is that translation, as well as the insuperable difficulty that inhabits its project, exposes certain tensions that pertain specifically to language: a possible incompatibility between proposition (*Satz*) and denomination (*Wort*) or between the literal and what he calls the symbolic meaning of a text or, within the symbolic dimension itself, between what is being symbolized and the symbolizing function. The conflict is stated, in most general terms, as existing between what language means (*das Gemeinte*) and the manner in which it produces meaning (*die Art des Meinens*). It is certainly true that, in Benjamin's essay and elsewhere in his writings, these tensions are, to some degree, suspended in what he refers to as pure language: *die reine Sprache*. But it is equally clear that this apparent transcendence does not occur in the realm of art but in that of the sacred. Between Benjamin's *reine Sprache* and Valéry's *poésie pure* there is very little in common. Far from being nostalgia or a prophecy of the sacred, poetic language, of which the inherent inadequacy is made explicit in its translation, is what has to be forgotten to find access to the sacred: in the poetic translations that Hölderlin made of Sophocles "meaning collapses from abyss to abyss, until it threatens to lose itself in the bottomless depths of language." In such a sentence, "abyss" should perhaps be read as technically and neutrally as in any trivial "mise en abyme." The existential pathos is counterbalanced by the fact that these "bottomless depths" of language are also its most manifest and ordinary grammatical dimensions, the specific linguistic categories that Benjamin can list with some precision. What this does to Benjamin's subsequent claims of transcendence (or to their perhaps fallacious understanding *as* transcendence) is not our present concern. It establishes, however, that as far as poetry and its history are concerned, there can be no question of essences. The rejection of a conception of poetry as message or reception is not the result of an essentialist conception of literature but of the critique of such a conception. With numerous qualifications, something similar could be said of Heidegger's essay "On the Origin of the Work of Art," which Jauss summarizes (and dismisses) as an assertion of a "timeless present" or a "self-sufficient presence" (p. 63) of the work of art, a simplification that does scant justice to Heidegger's dialectical concept of historical preservation (*Bewahrung*) on which Jauss himself, possibly by way of Gadamer, is dependent.

The point is not to oppose to each other philosophical traditions some of which Jauss could easily enlist on his side of the question. Rather, the reference to Benjamin's essay draws attention to the possibility that a concept such as "horizon of expectation" is not necessarily applicable, without further elaboration, to the arts of language. For all the obstacles to understanding mentioned by Benjamin belong specifically to language rather than to the phenomenal world; consequently, the expectation that they could be mastered by analogy with processes that stem from the psychology of perception is by no means certain. Husserl himself, among others, could be invoked to caution against the possibility of such a mistranslation.[15] The hermeneutics of experience and the hermeneutics of reading are not necessarily compatible. This does not imply that the solutions proposed by Jauss are inadequate or that the recourse to perception can or should be avoided altogether; the opposite is the case. It does mean, however, that the horizon of Jauss's methodology, like all methodologies, has limitations that are not accessible to its own analytical tools. The limitation, in this case, has to do with linguistic factors that threaten to interfere with the synthesizing power of the historical model. And it also means that these same factors will then exercise a more or less occult power over Jauss's own discourse, especially over the details of his textual interpretations.

At first sight, this hardly seems to be the case. Jauss is by no means adverse to taking the linguistic aspects of texts into consideration, nor is he in any way on the defensive in dealing with the work of linguists. His preference, however, goes to linguists who attempt to mediate between the communicative and the aesthetic function of language, to what one could call the stylists of communication theory. Jauss has argued from the start that the recognition of the formal and aesthetic aspects of a text are not to be separated from historical investigations having to do with its reception; a good formalist, by the strength of his own performance, has to become a historian. The Czech linguist Felix V. Vodička, whose work is often cited with approval by Jauss and other Konstanz theoreticians, has made this explicit in his conception of reception as the historical "concretization" of a linguistic structure. The element of negativity that, in Jauss's horizon of expectation, is located in the nonawareness of the background, resides, in Vodička and in the Prague linguists generally, in the characterization of literary language as a language of *signs*. Just as an element of not-knowing is built into the model of the horizon, the concept of literary sign implies an element of indeterminacy and of arbitrariness. In the words of Jan Mukařovský, a leading figure of the Prague Linguistic Circle, as quoted by Vodička: "Although the work of literature is closely dependent in its effect on communication by signs, it depends on it in such a manner that it is the dialectical negation of an actual communication."[16] The ensuing polysemy is mastered by inscribing it within the historical and social continuum of particular receptions or "concretizations." Structural aesthetics as practiced by the Prague circle are therefore far from being a threat to Jauss. His historical concepts seem to dovetail perfectly with their linguistic terminology. This theoretical alliance achieves a genuine synthesis between hermeneutics and poetics. Is this to say that Benjamin's anxieties about the semantics of poetic language are convincingly laid to rest by the concerted investigations of both linguists and historians?

The answer will depend on a term that until now we were able to keep in abeyance. When Vodička speaks of concretizations, he strongly insists that these are *aesthetic* concretizations, just as Jauss's reception is an *aesthetic* reception, in an *aesthetic* process. How "aesthetic" is to be understood here is not self-evident. For Mukařovský, the aesthetic quality of the work of literature, like its historical quality, is a function of its sign-structure. In the analysis of poetic diction "the structure of the linguistic sign holds the center of attention, whereas the (nonpoetic) functions are oriented toward extralinguistic instances and goals exceeding the linguistic sign."[17] The focus, in poetic texts, on the process of signification rather than on significance is what is said to be specifically aesthetic. The arbitrary and conventional aspects of the sign thus acquire value as aesthetic features and it is by this same conventionality that the collective, social, and historical dimensions of the work can be reintegrated. This is the very point at which the procedures of a historian such as Jauss and poeticians such as Vodička or Mukařovský converge. It is Jauss's considerable merit to have perceived and demonstrated the linkage between reception and semiotics. The condensation of literary history and structural analysis occurs by ways of the category of the aesthetic and depends for its possibility on the stability of this category.

This stability, however, remains problematic for many philosophers. A concatenation of the aesthetic with the meaning-producing powers of language is a strong temptation to the mind but, precisely for that reason, it also opens up a Pandora's box. The aesthetic is, by definition, a seductive notion that appeals to the pleasure principle, a eudaemonic judgment that can displace and conceal values of truth and falsehood likely to be more resilient to desire than values of pleasure and pain. Nietzsche, who is acutely aware of aesthetic powers as tools of the will, warns that judgments based on pleasure or on pain "are the silliest *expressions* of judgments imaginable — by which, of course, I [Nietzsche] do not mean to say that the judgments which become audible in this manner have to be silly."[18] Aesthetic reactions can never be considered as central causes (*Ursachen*) but only as trivial side-effects (*Nebensachen*): "they are value judgments *of the second order* which are derived from a centrally dominant value; they consider the useful and the harmful in a purely affective mode and are therefore absolutely volatile and dependent."[19] The considerable interest they hold for the historian or for the critical philosopher is symptomatological rather than systematic: they are philosophically significant to the extent that their power to mislead points to other causes. Hegel's massively misunderstood treatment of the aesthetic as a provisional (*vorläufig*, a word that also occurs in Benjamin[20]) form of cognition is entirely in the spirit of his continuators Kierkegaard and Nietzsche. This means, among other things, that whenever the aesthetic is invoked as an appeal to clarity and control, whenever, in other words, a symptom is made into a remedy for the disorder that it signals, a great deal of caution is in order. Jauss's straightforward equation of the aesthetic with the pleasure principle, as in the essay on Valéry and Goethe, or as is implicit in his subsequent book on *Aesthetic Experience and Literary Hermeneutics*[21], is in itself symptomatic. And when this same principle is then made to link up with the more objective properties of language revealed by linguistic analysis, the suspicion arises that aesthetic judgment has trespassed beyond its legitimate epistemological reach. As is to be expected in such a case, the traces of this transgression become noticeable by the omission, rather than by the misrepresentation, of certain features of language.

Characteristic of such omissions is Jauss's lack of interest, bordering on outright dismissal, in any considerations derived from what has, somewhat misleadingly, come to be known as the "play" of the signifier, semantic effects produced on the level of the letter rather than of the word or the sentence and which, therefore, escape from the network of hermeneutic questions and answers. Such a concern with "the instances of the letter" is particularly in evidence, as is well known, among certain French writers not generally included within Jauss's own critical canon of relevant *Fachliteratur*. He has always treated such Parisian extravagances with a measure of suspicion and even when, under the pressure of their persistence as well as of genuine affinities between their enterprise and his own, he has acknowledged some of their findings, it has always been a guarded and partial recognition. There are good pedagogical and ideological reasons, of local rather than general interest, for this reserve. The tactics of exclusion, on the other hand, are so familiar as to constitute, within the community of literary scholarship, a mass reaction: in a long tradition, more familiar even in the world of *haute couture* than of literary theory, what is made in Paris is often thought of as more fashionable than sound. What is in fashion in Paris is tolerable only as window display, not for everyday wear. Yet, as we know from Baudelaire, fashion, *la mode*, is itself a highly significant and, precisely, aesthetic and historical category that historians should not underestimate. When it becomes fashionable to dismiss fashion, clearly something interesting is going on, and what is being discarded as *mere* fashion must also be more insistent, and more threatening, than its frivolity and transcience would seem to indicate. What is being dismissed, in the context of our question, is the play of the signifier, the very same topic (if it can thus be called) which Friedrich Schlegel singled out when the displeasure of his readers, the accusation of frivolity, forced him, in 1800, to suspend publication of the *Athenäum*.[22]

In the practice of his own textual interpretation, Jauss pays little attention to the semantic play of the signifier and when, on rare occasions, he does so, the effect is quickly reaestheticized before anything unpleasant might occur — just as any word-play is so easily disarmed by assimilating it to the harmlessness of a mere pun or *calembour*. Thus, in a recent article that makes use of one of Baudelaire's *Spleen* poems as a textual example,[23] Jauss comments judiciously on the lines in which the name of the eighteenth-century painter Boucher is made to pseudo-rhyme with the word "débouché" (uncorked):

> . . . *un vieux boudoir*
> *Où les pastels plaintifs et les pâles Boucher,*
> *Seuls, respirent l'odeur d'un flacon débouché.*

In a rare Lacanian moment, Jauss suggests that what he calls a "grotesque" effect of verbal play — the rhyme-pair Boucher/débouché — is also something more uncanny: "The still harmonious representation of the last perfume escaping from the uncorked bottle overturns (*kippt um*) into the dissonant connotation of a 'decapitated' rococo painter Boucher" (p. 157). After having gone this far, it becomes very hard to stop. Should one not also notice that this bloody scene is made gorier still by the presence of a proper name (Boucher) which, as a common name, means butcher, thus making the "pâle Boucher" the agent of his own execution? This pale and white text of recollection (the first line of the poem is "J'ai plus de souvenirs que si j'avais mille ans") turns red with a brutality that takes us out of the inwardness of memory, the ostensible *theme* of the poem, into a very threatening literality to which an innocent art-term such as "dissonance" hardly does justice. Much more apt is Jauss's very concrete and indecorous, almost colloquial, word "umkippen" (to overturn), which "overturns" the beheaded Boucher as if he were himself an uncorked "flacon" spilling his blood. That this would happen to the proper name of a painter, and by means of a merely "grotesque" and frivolous play on words, tells us a great deal about the difficult-to-control borderline (or lack of it) between the aesthetics of *homo ludens* and the literal incisiveness of *Wortwitz*. For reasons of decorum, the gap that Jauss has opened, by his own observation, in the aesthetic texture of the language is at once reclosed, as if the commentator felt that he might betray the integrity of the text with which he is dealing.

This hesitation, this restraint before giving in to the coarseness and the potential violence of the signifier, is by no means to be condemned as a lack of boldness. After all, Baudelaire himself does not threaten us, or himself, directly, and by keeping the menace wrapped up, as it were, within a play of language, he does not actually draw blood. He seems to stop in time, to fence with a foil[24] — for how could anyone be hurt by a mere rhyme? Yet, the poetic restraint exercised by Baudelaire differs entirely from the aesthetic restraint exercised by Jauss. For the play on words, as we all know from obscene jokes, far from preserving decorum, dispenses with it quite easily, as Baudelaire dispensed with it to the point of attracting the attention of the *police des moeurs*. What it does not dispense with, unlike decorum (a classical and aesthetic concept), is the ambiguity of a statement that, because it is a verbal thrust and not an actual blow, allows itself to be taken figurally but, in so doing, opens up the way to the performance of what it only seems to feign or prefigure. The false rhyme on Boucher/débouché is a figure, a paronomasis. But only after we have, with the assistance of H. R. Jauss, noticed and recognized it as such, does the actual threat inherent in the fiction produced by the actual hands of the painter (who is also a butcher) become manifest. This no longer describes an aesthetic but a poetic structure, a structure that has to do with what Benjamin identified as a nonconvergence of "meaning" with "the devices that produce meaning," or what Nietzsche has in mind when he insists that eudaemonic judgments are inadequate "means of expression" of a cognition. Since this poetic (as distinguished from aesthetic) structure has to do with the necessity of deciding whether a statement in a text is to be taken as a figure or *à la lettre*, it pertains to rhetoric. In this particular instance, Jauss has come upon the rhetorical dimension of language; it is significant that he has to draw back in the face of his own discovery.

But how can it be said that Jauss swerves from the consideration of rhetoric where he has so many perceptive and relevant things to say about it, and does so without any trace of the restraint for which I am both praising and blaming him in his gloss on Baudelaire's poem? An extended study of his writings, going well beyond the decorous limits of an introduction, would show that something similar to what happens in the essay on "Spleen II" occurs whenever rhetorical categories are at stake. One hint may suffice. In a polemical exchange with Gadamer about the rhetoric of classicism (p. 30), classical art is assimilated to a rhetoric of mimesis (the Aristotelian rhetorical category par excellence), and opposed to medieval and modern art, which are said to be nonmimetic and nonrepresentational. A rhetorical trope serves as the ground of a historical system of periodization that allows for the correct understanding of meaning; once again, a poetic and a hermeneutic category have been seamlessly articulated. But if this assertion seems so reasonable, is it not because it corresponds to a received idea of literary history rather than being the result of a rigorous linguistic analysis? The alternative to *mimesis* would be, one assumes, allegory, which all of us associate with medieval and, at least since Benjamin, with modern art. If we then ask whether Jauss's own model for reading, the horizon of expectation, is classical or modern, one would have to say that it is the former. For it is certainly, like all hermeneutic systems, overwhelmingly mimetic; if literary understanding involves a horizon of expectation, it resembles a sense perception, and it will be correct to the precise extent that it "imitates" such a perception. The negativity inherent in the Husserlian model is a negativity within the sensory itself and not its negation, let alone its "other." It is impossible to conceive of a phenomenal experience that would not be mimetic, as it is impossible to conceive of an aesthetic judgment that would not be dependent on imitation as a constitutive category, also and especially when the judgment, as is the case in Kant, is interiorized as the consciousness of a subject. The concept of nonrepresentational art stems from painting and from a pictorial aesthetic that is firmly committed to the phenomenalism of art. The allegory, or allegoresis, which Jauss opposes to mimesis, remains firmly rooted in the classical phenomenalism of an aesthetics of representation.

"Allegory," however, is a loaded term that can have different implications. A reference to Walter Benjamin can again be helpful, all the more so since Jauss alludes to him in the same essay on Baudelaire from which I have been quoting. In his treatment of allegory Benjamin plays, by anticipation, the part of Hamann in a debate in which Jauss would be playing the part of Herder. For him, allegory is best compared to a commodity; it has, as he puts it in a term taken from Marx, *Warencharakter*, "matter that is death in a double sense and that is anorganic." The "anorganic" quality of allegory is, however, not equivalent, as Jauss's commentary seems to suggest (p. 179), to the negation of the natural world; the opposition between organic and anorganic, in Benjamin, is not like the opposition between *organisch* and *aorgisch* familiar from the terminology of idealist philosophy in Schelling and also in Hölderlin. The commodity is anorganic because it exists as a mere piece of paper, as an inscription or a notation on a certificate. The opposition is not between nature and consciousness (or subject) but between what exists as language and what does not. Allegory is material or materialistic, in Benjamin's sense, because its dependence on the letter, on the literalism of the letter, cuts it off sharply from symbolic and aesthetic syntheses. "The subject of allegory can only be called a grammatical subject"; the quotation is not from Benjamin but from one of the least valued sections of Hegel's *Lectures on Aesthetics*,[25] the canonical bible, still for Heidegger, of the phenomenalism of art. Allegory names the rhetorical process by which the literary text moves from a phenomenal, world-oriented to a grammatical, language-oriented direction. It thus also names the moment when aesthetic and poetic values part company. Everyone has always known that allegory, like the commodity and unlike aesthetic delight, is, as Hegel puts it, "icy and barren."[26] If this is so, can one then still share Jauss's confidence that "the allegorical intention, pursued to the utmost of *rigor mortis*, can still reverse (*umschlagen*) this extreme alienation into an appearance of the beautiful" (p. 205)?[27] If the return to the aesthetic is a turning away from the language of allegory and rhetoric, then it is also a turning away from literature, a breaking of the link between poetics and history.

The debate between Jauss and Benjamin on allegory is a debate between the classical position, here represented by Jauss, and a tradition[28] that undoes it, and that includes, in the wake of Kant, among others Hamann, Friedrich Schlegel, Kierkegaard, and Nietzsche. The debate occurs in the course of interpreting Baudelaire's poem "Spleen II." The poem deals with history as recollection, *souvenir*, Hegel's *Erinnerung*. Jauss's precise and suggestive reading carefully traces the manner in which an inner state of mind (spleen) is first compared to an outside object (ll. 2 and 5), then asserted to *be* such an object (l. 6), then becomes the voice of a speaking subject that declares itself to be an object (l. 8), and finally culminates (ll. 19-20) in the dialogical relationship of an apostrophe by this subject to a material object that has itself acquired consciousness:

— *Désormais tu n'es plus, ô matière vivante!*
Qu'un granit entouré d'une vague épouvante. . . .

At the conclusion of the poem (ll. 22-24), the enigmatic figure of "Un vieux sphinx" appears and is said, however restrictively and negatively, to be singing:

Un vieux sphinx . . .
Ne chante qu'aux rayons du soleil qui se couche.

Jauss convincingly identifies this sphinx as the figure of the poetic voice and his song as the production of the text of "Spleen II" (pp. 169, 170). We rediscover the not unfamiliar, specular (that is to say solar and phenomenal) conception of a "poetry of poetry,"[29] the self-referential text that thematizes its own invention, prefigures its own reception, and achieves, as aesthetic cognition and pleasure, the recovery from the most extreme of alienations, from the terror of encrypted death. "The dissonance of the statement is aesthetically harmonized by the assonance and the balance between the various textual layers" (p. 182). "In a successfully elaborated form, the literary representation of terror and anxiety is always already, thanks to aesthetic sublimation, overcome" (p. 167). The promise of aesthetic sublimation is powerfully argued, in a manner that leaves little room for further questioning.

The assurance that further questioning nevertheless should take place has little to do with one's own spleen, with pessimism, nihilism or the historical necessity to overcome alienation. It depends on powers of poetic analysis, which it is in no one's power to evade. One of the thematic textual "layers" of "Spleen II" that remains constant throughout the text is that of the mind as a hollow container, box, or grave and the transformation of this container, or of the corpse contained in it, into a voice:

> . . . *mon triste cerveau.*
> *C'est une pyramide, un immense caveau,*
> *Qui contient plus de morts que la fosse commune.*
> *— Je suis un cimetière abhorré de la lune,*
>
> . . . .
> *— Désormais tu n'es plus, ô matière vivante!*
> *Qu'un granit entouré d'une vague épouvante,*
> *Assoupi dans le fond d'un Saharah brumeux;*
> *Un vieux sphinx ignoré du monde insoucieux,*
> *Oublié sur la carte, et dont l'humeur farouche*
> *Ne chante qu'aux rayons du soleil qui se couche.*

The transformation occurs as one moves from mind (as recollection) to pyramid and to sphinx. It occurs, in other words, by an itinerary that travels by way of Egypt. Egypt, in Hegel's *Aesthetics*, is the birthplace of truly symbolic art, which is monumental and architectural, not literary. It is the art of memory that remembers death, the art of history as *Erinnerung*. The emblem for interiorized memory, in Hegel, is that of the buried treasure or mine (*Schacht*), or, perhaps, a well.[30] Baudelaire, however, fond though he is of well-metaphors, uses "pyramid," which connotes, of course, Egypt, monument and crypt, but which also connotes, to a reader of Hegel, the emblem of the sign as opposed to the symbol.[31] The sign, which pertains specifically to language and to rhetoric, marks, in Hegel, the passage from sheer inward recollection and imagination to thought (*Denken*), which occurs by way of the deliberate forgetting of substantial, aesthetic, and pictorial symbols.[32] Baudelaire, who in all likelihood never heard of Hegel, happens to hit on the same emblematic sequence[33] to say something very similar. The decapitated painter lies, as a corpse, in the crypt of recollection and is replaced by the sphinx, who, since he has a head and a face, can be apostrophized in the poetic speech of rhetorical figuration. But the sphinx is not an emblem of recollection but, like Hegel's sign, an emblem of forgetting. In Baudelaire's poem he is not just "oublié" but "oublié sur la carte," inaccessible to memory because he is imprinted on paper, because he is himself the inscription of a sign. Contrary to Jauss's assertion — "for who could say with more right than the sphinx: j'ai plus de souvenirs que si j'avais mille ans" — the sphinx is the one least able to say anything of the sort. He is the grammatical subject cut off from its consciousness, the poetic analysis cut off from its hermeneutic function, the dismantling of the aesthetic and pictorial world of "le soleil qui se couche" by the advent of poetry as allegory. What he "sings" can never be the poem entitled "Spleen"; his song is not the sublimation but the forgetting, by inscription, of terror, the dismemberment of the aesthetic whole into the unpredictable play of the literary letter. We could not have reached this understanding without the assistance of Jauss's reading. His work confronts us with the enigma of the relationship betwen the aesthetic and the poetic and, by so doing, it demonstrates the rigor of its theoretical questioning.

Notes

1. "Reading and History" originally appeared as the introduction to Hans Robert Jauss, *Toward an Aesthetic of Reception* (Minneapolis: University of Minnesota Press, 1982). All further page references are given in the text.

2. H. R. Jauss's first full-length book is a study of the narrative structure of Marcel Proust's *A la recherche du temps perdu*, well ahead of its time and all too little known outside Germany: *Zeit und Erinnerung in Marcel Prousts 'A la recherche du temps perdu': Ein Beitrag zur Theorie des Romans* (Heidelberg: C. Winter, 1955).

3. The term was coined by Stanley Fish in an article that goes back to 1970 published in *New Literary History*. Fish later stated that it was "not the happiest of designations" for reasons, however, that have little to do with the point stressed here. For a good brief survey of reader-response criticism in the United States, see Leopold Damrosch, Jr., ("Samuel Johnson and Reader-Response Criticism," in *The Eighteenth Century, Theory and Interpretation* XXI, 2 (Spring 1980), pp. 91-108) who quotes Fish. Anthologies of reader-response criticism such as, among others, *The Reader in the Text: Essays on Audience and Interpretation*, ed. Susan Suleiman and Inge Crossman (Princeton: Princeton University Press, 1980) have recently been published in this country.

4. Rainer Warning, ed., *Rezeptionsästhetik: Theorie und Praxis* (Munich, 1975).

5. The sequence of volumes containing the proceedings of the yearly meetings of the research group have appeared since 1963 under the general title *Poetik und Hermeneutik*.

6. See, for example, Martin Heidegger's introductory statement in *Erläuterungen zu Hölderlins Dichtung* (Frankfurt am Main: Klostermann, 1951), p. 8.

7. Aristotle, *Rhetoric*, p. 1406b.

8. Rainer Warning, "Rezeptionsästhetik als literaturwissenschaftliche Pragmatik," in *Rezeptionsästhetik*, p. 25.

9. Jauss directly refers to Bloom in the essay "Goethe's and Valéry's Faust: On the Hermeneutics of Question and Answer," in *Toward an Aesthetic of Reception*, trans. Timothy Bahti (Minneapolis: University of Minnesota Press, 1982), pp. 114, 122.

10. See, for instance, Edmund Hussérl, *Ideas: General Introduction to Phenomenology*, trans. W. R. Boyce Gibson (New York: Humanities Press, 1969) sections 27, 28, 44, 47.

11. The German "ungedacht" or the French "impensé" would be better terms, not available in English.

12. "Silhouetted" approximately translates the Husserlian term "Abschattung."

13. Walter Benjamin, "Die Aufgabe des Übersetzers" in *Illuminationen* (Frankfurt: Suhrkamp, 1961), p. 56.

14. Warning, *Rezeptionsästhetik*, p. 9.

15. See Husserl, *Logical Investigations*, trans. J. N. Findlay (London: Routledge & Kegan Paul, 1970), Vol. II; also J. P. Schobinger, *Variationen zu Walter Benjamins Sprachmeditationen*, (Basel/ Stuttgart: Schwabe, 1979), p. 102, and Jacques Derrida, *La voix et le phénomène* (Paris: Presses Universitaires de France, 1967), especially chapter VII, "Le supplément d'origine," pp. 98-117.

16. Warning, *Rezeptionsästhetik*, p. 89.

17. Jan Mukařovský, *The Word and Verbal Art*, trans. John Burbank and Peter Steiner, with a foreword by René Wellek (New Haven: Yale University Press, 1977), p. 68.

18. Friedrich Nietzsche, "Nachlass," in *Werke in drei Bänden*, ed. Karl Schlechta (Munich: Carl Hauser, 1956), III, p. 683.

19. *Ibid.*, III, p. 685.

20. Benjamin, *Illuminationen*, p. 62: "Damit ist allerdings zugestanden, dass alle Übersetzung nur eine irgendwie *vorläufige* Art ist, sich mit der Fremdheit der Sprachen auseinanderzusetzen."

21. H. R. Jauss, *Aesthetic Experience and Literary Hermeneutics*, trans. Michael Shaw (Minneapolis: University of Minnesota Press, 1982).

22. Friedrich Schlegel, "Über die Unverständlichkeit" in *Kritische Schriften*, ed. Wolfdietrich Rasch (Munich: Carl Hauser, 1970), pp. 530-42.

23. H. R. Jauss, "The Poetic Text Within the Change of Horizons of Reading: The Example of Baudelaire's 'Spleen II'." in *Toward an Aesthetic of Reception*, pp. 139-85.

24. In "Über einige Motive bei Baudelaire," *Illuminationen*. p. 210, Benjamin quotes the lines from another of the *Fleurs du Mal* poems:

> Je vais m'exercer seul à ma fantasque escrime,
> Flairant dans tous les coins les hasards de la rime. . . .
>
> ("Le Soleil")

25. *Vorlesungen über die Ästhetik* (Frankfurt am Main: Suhrkamp, Theorie Werkausgabe, 1970), vol. 13, p. 512.

26. *Ibid.*, p. 512.

27. "*Erscheinung des Schönen*" is, of course, the traditional Hegelian vocabulary for the aesthetic experience. The "umkippen" of Jauss's earlier, corrosive observation on Baudelaire's play on Boucher/débouche, which suggests the demolition of the aesthetic idol as if it were the *colonne Vendôme* or any monument honoring a tyrant, is now replaced by the more dignified "umschlagen." Taken literally, however, *schlagen* (to beat) in the cliché *umschlagen* is rather more threatening than *kippen* (to tilt).

28. The use of "tradition" in this context is one of the numerous occasions in which one can share Rousseau's naive regret that we have no diacritical mark at our disposal by which to indicate

irony. It also indicates that, try as I may, when I seem to be reproaching Jauss for not freeing himself from classical constraints, I am not more liberated from them than he is.

29. "Poesie der Poesie" is a concept frequently developed in connection with Paul Valéry, whose authority as a poetician is, for various and complex reasons, overrated in Germany. The "Valérization" of Mallarmé and of Baudelaire is a case in which Harold Bloom's notion of belatedness would have a salutary effect.

30. *Enzyklopädie der philosophischen Wissenschaften* (Frankfurt am Main: Suhrkamp, Theorie Werkausgabe, 1970), vol. 10, section 453, p. 260.

31. *Ibid.*, section 458, p. 270.

32. *Ibid.*, section 464, p. 282.

33. That the coincidence may be due to common occult sources in Hegel and Baudelaire obscures rather than explains the passage. It distracts the reader from wondering why the use of this particular emblematic code can be "right" in a lyric poem as well as in a philosophical treatise.

Conclusions: Walter Benjamin's "The Task of the Translator"

I at first thought to leave this last session open for conclusions and discussion; I still hope for the discussion, but I have given up on the conclusions. It seemed to me best, rather than trying to conclude (which is always a terrible anticlimax), just to repeat once more what I have been saying since the beginning, using another text in order to have still another version, another formulation of some of the questions with which we have been concerned throughout this series. It seemed to me that this text by Benjamin on "The Task of the Translator" is a text that is very well known, both in the sense that it is very widely circulated, and in the sense that in the profession you are nobody unless you have said something about this text. Since probably most of us have tried to say something about it, let me see what I can do, and since some of you may be well ahead

---

What appears here is an edited transcript of the last of six Messenger Lectures delivered at Cornell University in February and March of 1983. Allusions to the preceding lectures may be clarified by reference to the published essays "Hegel on the Sublime" and "Phenomenality and Materiality in Kant," and to the forthcoming "Kant and Schiller." This text is based on tape recordings supplemented with eight pages of rough manuscript notes. Solecisms and redundancies have been retained where the possibility of foregrounding a gap between oral performance and printed text seemed to outweigh the likelihood of inconvenience to the reader. In punctuating I have tried to reproduce the pace of oral delivery and to close off as few readings as possible, even when leaving ambiguities open may have been less true to de Man's intent than to my own reluctance to render a "definitive" text. Except for a few passages in which de Man adopts Harry Zohn's translation, quotations reproduce de Man's own impromptu translations. The notes are my own. Thanks to Cornell's Uris Library and to Christopher Fynsk for tapes, and to Roger Blood for help in transcribing. — William Jewett

of me, I look forward to the questions or suggestions you may have. So, far from concluding or from making very general statements, I want to stay pretty close to this particular text, and see what comes out. If I say stay close to the text, since it is a text on translation, I will need — and that is why I have all these books — translations of this text, because if you have a text which says it is impossible to translate, it is very nice to see what happens when that text gets translated. And the translations confirm, brilliantly, beyond any expectations which I may have had, that it is impossible to translate, as you will see in a moment.

Nevertheless, I have placed this within a kind of framework, a framework which is historical. Since the problems of history have come up frequently, I thought it would be good to situate it within a historical or pseudohistorical framework, and then to move on from there. Therefore I start out with a recurrent problem in history and historiography, which is the problem of modernity. I use as an introduction into this a little essay by the German philosopher Gadamer, who in a collection called *Aspekte der Modernität* wrote, many years ago, interesting articles called "Die philosophischen Grundlagen des zwanzigsten Jahrhunderts" ("The Philosophical Foundations of the Twentieth Century"). Gadamer asks the somewhat naive but certainly relevant question, whether what is being done in philosophy in the twentieth century differs essentially from what was being done before, and if it then makes sense to speak of a modernity in philosophical speculation in the twentieth century. He finds as the general theme, the general enterprise of contemporary philosophy, a critical concern with the concept of the subject. Perhaps one wouldn't say this now, which perhaps dates this piece a little bit, but it is still relevant. His question then is whether the way in which the critique of the concept of the subject is being addressed by present-day philosophy differs essentially from the way it had been addressed by the predecessors of contemporary philosophy, in German Idealist philosophy — in some of the authors with whom we have been concerned, such as Kant, Hegel, and others. He writes the following sentence, which is our starting point:

> Is the critique of the concept of the subject which is being attempted in
> our century something else, something different from a mere repetition of
> what had been accomplished by German Idealist philosophy — and, must
> we not admit, with, in our case, incomparably less power of abstraction,
> and without the conceptual strength that characterized the earlier
> movement?[1]

Is what we are doing just a repetition? And he answers, surprise: "This is not the case." What we are doing really is something new, something different, and we can lay claim to being modern philosophers. He finds three rubrics in which we — contemporary philosophers — he, Gadamer — is ahead of his predecessors, and he characterizes these three progressions in terms of a decreased naiveté. To us now it seems, if we look back on Hegel or Kant, that there is a certain naiveté there which we have now grown beyond. He distinguishes between three types of naiveté, which he calls *Naivität des Setzens* (naiveté of positing), *Naivität der Reflexion* (naiveté of reflection), and *Naivität des Begriffs* (naiveté of the concept).

Very briefly, what is meant by the first, by a certain "naiveté of position," is a critique which we have been able to develop of pure perception and of pure declarative discourse, in relation to the problem of the subject. We are now ahead of Hegel in that we know better that the subject does not dominate its own utterances; we are more aware that it is naive to assume that the subject really controls its own discourse; we know this is not the case. Yet he qualifies this one bit: nevertheless, understanding is available to us to some extent, by a hermeneutic process in which understanding, by a historical process, can catch up with the presuppositions it had made about itself. We get a development of Gadamer, disciple of Heidegger, of the notion of a hermeneutic circle, where the subject is blind to its own utterance, but where nevertheless the reader who is aware of the historicity of that blindness can recover the meaning, can recover a certain amount of control over the text by means of this particular hermeneutic pattern. This model of understanding is ahead of the Hegelian model exactly to the same extent that one could say that the hermeneutics of Heidegger are ahead of the hermeneutics of Hegel, in Gadamer's sense.

He then speaks of the "naiveté of reflection," and develops further what is already posited in the first; namely, he asserts the possibility now of a historicity of understanding, in a way that is not accessible to individual self-reflection. It is said that Hegel, in a sense, was not historical enough, that in Hegel it is still too much the subject itself which originates its own understanding, whereas now one is more aware of the difficulty of the relationship between the self and its discourse. Where in the first progression he refers to Heidegger's contribution, here he refers very much to his own contribution — historicizing the notion of understanding, by seeing understanding (as the later *Rezeptionsästhetik*, which comes from Gadamer to a large extent, will develop it) as a process between author and reader in which the reader acquires an understanding of the text by becoming aware of the historicity of the movement that occurs between the text and himself. Here Gadamer also makes a claim that something new is going on nowadays, and indeed, the stress on reception, the stress on reading, are characteristic of contemporary theory, and can be claimed to be new.

Finally, he speaks of the "naiveté of the concept," in which the problem of the relationship between philosophical discourse and rhetorical and other devices which pertain more to the realm of ordinary discourse or common language was not, with Kant and Hegel, being examined critically. We alluded to an example of that yesterday when Kant raises the problem of *hypotyposis* and invites us to become aware of the use of metaphors in our own philosophical discourse. That type of question, which at least was mentioned by Kant, and was mentioned much less by Hegel, is now much more developed. Gadamer's allusion is to Wittgenstein, and also indirectly to Nietzsche. We no longer think, says Gadamer, that conceptual and ordinary language are separable; we now have a concept of the problematics of language which is less naive in that it sees to what extent philosophical language is still dependent on ordinary language, and how close it is to it. This is the modernity which he suggests, and which he details by these three indications.

Now although this is Kantian to some extent in its critical outlook, it is still very much a Hegelian model. The scheme or concept of modernity as the overcoming of a certain non-awareness or naiveté by means of a critical negation — by means of a critical examination which implies the negation of certain positive relationships and the achieving of a new consciousness — allows for the establishment of a new discourse which claims to overcome or to renew a certain problematic. This pattern is very traditionally Hegelian, in the sense that the development of consciousness is always shown as a kind of overcoming of a certain naiveté and a rise of consciousness to another level. It is traditionally Hegelian, which does not mean that it is in Hegel, but it is in Hegel the way Hegel is being taught in the schools. Indeed, Gadamer ends his piece with a reference to Hegel:

> The concept of spirit, which Hegel borrowed from the Christian spiritual tradition, is still the ground of the critique of the subject and of the subjective spirit that appears as the main task of the post-Hegelian, that is to say modern, period. This concept of spirit (*Geist*), which transcends the subjectivity of the ego, finds its true abode in the phenomenon of language, which stands more and more as the center of contemporary philosophy.[2]

Contemporary philosophy is a matter of getting beyond Hegel in Hegelian terms, by focusing the Hegelian *démarche*, the Hegelian dialectic, more specifically on the question of language. That is how modernity is here defined, as a Hegelianism which has concentrated more on linguistic dimensions.

If we compare the critical, dialectical, non-essentialist (because pragmatic to some extent, since an allowance is made for common language) concept of modernity which Gadamer here advances, with Benjamin's text on language in "The Task of the Translator," then at first sight, Benjamin would appear as highly regressive. He would appear as messianic, prophetic, religiously messianic, in a way that may well appear to be a relapse into the naiveté denounced by Gadamer. Indeed, he has been criticized for this. Such a relapse would actually return to a much earlier stage even than that of Kant, Hegel, and idealist philosophy. The first impression you receive of Benjamin's text is that of a messianic, prophetic pronouncement, which would be very remote from the cold critical spirit which, from Hegel to Gadamer, is held up as the spirit of modernity. Indeed, as you read this text, you will have been struck by the messianic tone, by a figure of the poet as an almost sacred figure, as a figure which echoes sacred language. All references to particular poets within the text put this much in evidence. The poets who are being mentioned are poets one associates with a sacerdotal, an almost priestlike, spiritual function of poetry: this is true of Hölderlin, of George, and of Mallarmé, all of whom are very much present in the essay.

(Since I mention George, one is aware of the presence of George — a name which has now lost much of its significance, but which at that time in Germany was still considered the most important, central poet, although in 1923 or 1924 when this was written this was already getting toward its end. For example, Benjamin quotes Pannwitz, a disciple of George, at the end of the text. And he refers to George in a relevant way: in George there was a claim made for the poet, again, as some kind of prophet, as a kind of messianic figure — George doesn't kid around with that, he sees himself at least as Virgil and Dante combined into one, with still quite a bit added to it if necessary — therefore he has a highly exalted notion of the role of the poet, and incidentally of himself, and of the benefits that go with it. But this tone hangs over the German academic discourse and over a certain concept of poetry which were then current. There are many echoes of it in the way Benjamin approaches the problem, at least superficially seen. The same is true of references to Hölderlin, who at that time was a discovery of George and of his group, where you find a certain messianic, spiritual concept of Hölderlin. Many echoes of this are still to be found in Heidegger, who after all dedicated his commentaries on Hölderlin to Norbert von Hellingrath, who was a disciple of George and a member of the George circle, and who was, as you know, the first editor of Hölderlin. I sketch in this little piece of background — it may be familiar to you, it may be entirely redundant — to show that the mood, the atmosphere in which this essay was written is one in which the notion of the poetic as the sacred, as the language of the sacred, the figure of the poet as somehow a sacred figure, is common, and is frequent.)

It is not just in the form of echoes that this is present in Benjamin, it almost seems to have been part of the statement itself. This notion of poetry as the sacred, ineffable language finds perhaps its extreme form already from the beginning, in the categorical way in which Benjamin dismisses any notion of poetry as being oriented, in any sense, toward an audience or a reader. This passage has provoked the ire of the defenders of *Rezeptionsästhetik*, who analyze the problem of poetic interpretation from the perspective of the reader — Stanley Fish or Riffaterre in this country follow that line to some extent, but it is of course Jauss and his disciples who do this the most. For them, a sentence like the one which begins this essay is absolutely scandalous. Benjamin begins the essay by saying:

In the appreciation of a work of art or an art form, consideration of the receiver never proves fruitful. Not only is any reference to a certain public or its representatives misleading, but even the concept of an "ideal" receiver is detrimental in the theoretical consideration of art, since all it posits is the existence and nature of man as such. Art, in the same way, posits man's physical and spiritual existence, but in none of its works is it concerned with his response. No poem is intended for the reader, no picture for the beholder, no symphony for the listener.[3]

He couldn't be more categorical than in this assertion at the beginning of the essay. You can see how this would have thrown them into a slight panic in Konstanz, a panic with which they deal by saying that this is an essentialist theory of art, that this stress on the author at the expense of the reader is pre-Kantian, since already Kant had given the reader (the receptor, the beholder) an important role, more important than the author's. This is then held up as an example of the regression to a messianic conception of poetry which would be religious in the wrong sense, and it is very much attacked for that reason.

But, on the other hand, Benjamin is also frequently praised as the one who has returned the dimension of the sacred to literary language, and who has thus overcome, or at least considerably refined, the secular historicity of literature on which the notion of modernity depends. If one can think of modernity as it is described by Gadamer, as a loss of the sacred, as a loss of a certain type of poetic experience, as its replacement by a secular historicism which loses contact with what was originally essential, then one can praise Benjamin for having re-established the contact with what had there been forgotten. Even in Habermas there are statements in that direction. But closer to home, an example of somebody who reads Benjamin with a great deal of subtlety, who is aware of the complications, and who praises him precisely for the way in which he combines a complex historical pattern with a sense of the sacred, is Geoffrey Hartman, who writes in one of his latest books as follows:

> This chiasmus of hope and catastrophe is what saves hope from being unmasked as only catastrophe: as an illusion or unsatisfied movement of desire that wrecks everything. The foundation of hope becomes remembrance; which confirms the function, even the duty of historian and critic. To recall the past is a political act: a "recherche" that involves us with images of peculiar power, images that may constrain us to identify with them, that claim the "*weak* Messianic power" in us (Thesis 2). These images, split off from their fixed location in history, undo concepts of homogeneous time, flash up into or reconstitute the present. "To Robespierre," Benjamin writes, continuing Marx's reflections in *The Eighteenth Brumaire*, "ancient Rome was a past charged with the time of now (*Jetztzeit*) which he blasted out of the continuum of history. The French revolution viewed itself as Rome incarnate" (Thesis 14).[4]

The reference here is to historical remembrance, to a historical concept which then dovetails, which injects itself into an apocalyptic, religious, spiritual concept, thus marrying history with the sacred in a way which is highly seductive, highly attractive. It is certainly highly attractive to Hartman, and one can understand why, since it gives one both the language of despair, the language of nihilism, with the particular rigor that goes with that; but, at the same time, hope! So you have it all: you have the critical perception, you have the possibility of carrying on in apocalyptic tones, you have the particular eloquence that comes with that (because one can only really get excited if one writes in an apocalyptic mode); but you can still talk in terms of hope, and Benjamin would be an example of this combination of nihilistic rigor with sacred revelation. A man who likes a judicious, balanced perspective on those things, like Hartman, has reason to quote and to admire this possibility in Benjamin. The problem of the reception of Benjamin centers on this problem of the messianic, and very frequently it is this text on "The Task of the Translator" that is quoted as one of the most characteristic indicators in that direction.

We now then ask the simplest, the most naive, the most literal of possible questions in relation to Benjamin's text, and we will not get beyond that: what does Benjamin say? What does he say, in the most immediate sense possible? It seems absurd to ask a question that is so simple, that seems to be so unnecessary, because we can certainly admit that among literate people we would at least have some minimal agreement about what is being said here, allowing us then to embroider upon this statement, to take positions, discuss, interpret, and so on. But it seems that, in the case of this text, this is very difficult to establish. Even the translators, who certainly are close to the text, who had to read it closely to some extent, don't seem to have the slightest idea of what Benjamin is saying; so much so that when Benjamin says certain things rather simply in one way — for example he says that something is *not* — the translators, who at least know German well enough to know the difference between something *is* and something *is not*, don't see it! and put absolutely and literally the opposite of what Benjamin has said. This is remarkable, because the two translators I have — Harry Zohn, who translated the text in English, and Maurice de Gandillac, who translated the text in French — are very good translators, and know German very well. Harry Zohn, you may know; Maurice de Gandillac is an eminent professor of philosophy at the University of Paris, a very learned man who knows German very well, and who should be able to tell the difference between, for example, "Ich gehe nach Paris" and "Ich gehe nicht nach Paris." It is not more difficult than that, but somehow he doesn't get it.

An example which has become famous and has an anecdote is the passage near the end of Benjamin's essay, where Benjamin says the following: "Wo der Text unmittelbar, ohne vermittelnden Sinn," and so on, "der Wahrheit oder der Lehre angehört, ist er übersetzbar schlechthin" (p. 62). "Where the text pertains directly, without mediation, to the realm of the truth and of dogma, it is, without further ado, translatable" — the text can be translated, *schlechthin*, so there is no problem about translating it. Gandillac — I won't comment on this — translates this relatively simple, enunciatory sentence: "Là où le texte, immédiatement, sans l'entremise d'un sens . . . relève de la vérité ou de la doctrine, il est purement et simplement *in*traduisible" (p. 275) — *un*translatable. What adds some comedy to this particular instance is that Jacques Derrida was doing a seminar with this particular text in Paris, using the French — Derrida's German is pretty good, but he prefers to use the French, and when you are a philosopher in France you take Gandillac more or less seriously. So Derrida was basing part of his reading on the "intraduisible," on the untranslatability, until somebody in his seminar (so I'm told) pointed out to him that the correct word was "translatable." I'm sure Derrida could explain that it was the same . . . and I mean that in a positive sense, it *is* the same, but still, it is not the same without some additional explanation. This is an example, and we will soon see some other examples which are more germane to the questions which we will bring up about this text.

Why, in this text, to begin with, is the translator the exemplary figure? Why is the translator held up in relation to the very general questions about the nature of poetic language which the text asks? The text is a poetics, a theory of poetic language, so why does Benjamin not go to the poets? or to the reader, possibly; or the pair poet-reader, as in the model of reception? And since he is so negative about the notion of reception anyway, what makes the essential difference between the pair author-reader and the pair author-translator? There are, to some extent, obvious empirical answers one can give. The essay was written, as you know, as an introduction to Benjamin's own translation of the *Tableaux parisiens* of Baudelaire; it might just be out of megalomania that he selects the figure of the translator. But this is not the case. One of the reasons why he takes the translator rather than the poet is that the translator, per definition, fails. The translator can never do what the original text did. Any translation is always second in relation to the original, and the translator as such is lost from the very beginning. He is per definition underpaid, he is per definition overworked, he is per definition the one history will not really retain as an equal, unless he also happens to be a poet, but that is not always the case. If the text is called "Die Aufgabe des Übersetzers," we have to read this title more or less as a tautology: *Aufgabe*, task, can also mean the one who has to give up. If you enter the Tour de France and you give up, that is the *Aufgabe* — "er hat aufgegeben," he doesn't continue in the race anymore. It is in that sense also the defeat, the giving up, of the translator. The translator has to give up in relation to the task of refinding what was there in the original.

The question then becomes why this failure with regard to an original text, to an original poet, is for Benjamin exemplary. The question also becomes how the translator differs from the poet, and here Benjamin is categorical in asserting that the translator is unlike, differs essentially from, the poet and the artist. This is a curious thing to say, a thing that goes against common sense, because one assumes (and obviously it is the case) that some of the qualities necessary for a good translator are similar to the qualities necessary for a good poet. This does not mean therefore that they are doing the same thing. The assertion is so striking, so shocking in a way, that here again the translator (Maurice de Gandillac) does not see it. Benjamin says (in Zohn's translation): "Although translation, *unlike* art, cannot claim permanence for its products . . ." (p. 75); Gandillac, the same passage: "Ainsi la traduction, encore qu'elle ne puisse élever une prétention à la durée de ses ouvrages, et en cela elle *n'est pas sans ressemblance* avec l'art . . ." (p. 267). The original is absolutely unambiguous: "Übersetzung also, wiewohl sie auf Dauer ihrer Gebilde nicht Anspruch erheben kann and hierin *unähnlich* der Kunst . . ." (p. 55). As you come upon it in a text, the statement is so surprising, goes so much against common sense, that an intelligent, learned, and careful translator cannot see it, cannot see what Benjamin says. It is remarkable. Zohn saw it — don't get the impression that Zohn gets it all right and Gandillac gets it all wrong — basically Gandillac is a little ahead of Zohn, I think, in the final analysis.

At any rate, for Benjamin there is a sharp distinction between them. It is not necessary for good translators to be good poets. Some of the best translators — he mentions Voss (translator of Homer), Luther, and Schlegel — are very poor poets. There are some poets who are also translators: he mentions Hölderlin, and George, who translated Baudelaire — Dante also, but primarily Baudelaire, so Benjamin is close to George. But then, he says, it is not because they are great poets that they are great translators, they are great poets *and* they are great translators. They are not purely, as Heidegger will say of Hölderlin, *Dichter der Dichter*, but they are *Übersetzer der Dichter*, they are beyond the poets because they are also translators.

> A number of the most eminent ones, such as Luther, Voss, and Schlegel, are incomparably more important as translators than as creative writers; some of the great among them, such as Hölderlin and Stefan George, cannot be simply subsumed as poets, and quite particularly not if we consider them as translators. As translation is a mode of its own, the task of the translator, too, may be regarded as distinct and clearly differentiated from the task of the poet. (p. 76)

Of the differences between the situation of the translator and that of the poet, the first that comes to mind is that the poet has some relationship to meaning, to a statement that is not purely within the realm of language. That is the naiveté of the poet, that he has to say something, that he has to convey a meaning which does not necessarily relate to language. The relationship of the translator to the original is the relationship between language and language, wherein the problem of meaning or the desire to say something, the need to make a statement, is entirely absent. Translation is a relation from language to language, not a relation to an extralinguistic meaning that could be copied, paraphrased, or imitated. That is not the case for the poet; poetry is certainly not paraphrase, clarification, or interpretation, a copy in that sense; and that is already the first difference.

If it is in some fundamental way unlike poetry, what, in Benjamin's text, does translation resemble? One of the things it resembles would be philosophy, in that it is critical, in the same way that philosophy is critical, of a simple notion of imitation, of philosophical discourse as an *Abbild* (imitation, paraphrase, reproduction) of the real situation. Philosophy is not an imitation of the world as we know it, but it has another relationship to that world. Critical philosophy, and the reference would be specifically to Kant again, will be critical in the same way of the notion of the imitative concept of the world.

Um das echte Verhältnis zwischen Original und Übersetzung zu erfassen, ist eine Erwägung anzustellen, deren Absicht durchaus den Gedanken-gängen analog ist, in denen die Erkenntniskritik die Unmöglichkeit einer Abbildstheorie zu erweisen hat. (p. 53)

In order to seize upon the real relationship between the original and its translation, we must start a reflection of which the intent is in general similar to modes of thought by means of which a critical epistemology [there's Kant, *Erkenntniskritik*] demonstrates the impossibility of a theory of simple imitation.

Kant would indeed be critical of a notion of art as imitation; this would be true of Hegel to some extent too, because there is, precisely, a critical element that intervenes here and which takes this image, this model, away, which destroys, undoes this concept of imitation.

Translation is also, says Benjamin, more like criticism or like the theory of literature than like poetry itself. It is by defining himself in relation to Friedrich Schlegel and to German Romanticism in general that Benjamin establishes this similarity between literary criticism (in the sense of literary theory) and transla-tion; and this historical reference to the Jena Romanticism here gives to the notion of criticism and literary theory a dignity which it does not necessarily normally have. Both criticism and translation are caught in the gesture which Benjamin calls ironic, a gesture which undoes the stability of the original by giving it a definitive, canonical form in the translation or in the theorization. In a curious way, translation canonizes its own version more than the original was canonical. That the original was not purely canonical is clear from the fact that it demands translation; it cannot be definitive since it can be translated. But you cannot, says Benjamin, translate the translation; once you have a translation you cannot translate it any more. You can translate only an original. The translation canonizes, freezes, an original and shows in the original a mobility, an instability, which at first one did not notice. The act of critical, theoretical reading performed by a critic like Friedrich Schlegel and performed by literary theory in general — by means of which the original work is not imitated or reproduced but is to some extent put in motion, de-canonized, questioned in a way which undoes its claim to canonical authority — is similar to what a translator performs.

Finally, translation is like history, and that will be the most difficult thing to understand. In what is the most difficult passage in this text, Benjamin says that it is like history to the extent that history is not to be understood by analogy with any kind of natural process. We are not supposed to think of history as ripening, as organic growth, or even as a dialectic, as anything that resembles a natural process of growth and of movement. We are to think of history rather in the reverse way: we are to understand natural changes from the perspective of history, rather than understand history from the perspective of natural changes. If we want to understand what ripening is, we should understand it from the perspective of historical change. In the same way, the relationship between the translation and the original is not to be understood by analogy with natural processes such as resemblance or derivation by formal analogy; rather we are to understand the original from the perspective of the translation. To understand this historical pattern would be the burden of any reading of this particular text.

All these activities that have been mentioned — philosophy as critical epistemology, criticism and literary theory (the way Friedrich Schlegel does it), or history understood as a nonorganic process — are themselves derived from original activities. Philosophy derives from perception, but it is unlike perception because it is the critical examination of the truth-claims of perception. Criticism derives from poetry because it is inconceivable without the poetry that precedes it. History derives from pure action, since it follows necessarily upon acts which have already taken place. Because all these activities are derived from original activities, they are therefore singularly inconclusive, are failed, are aborted in a sense from the start because they are derived and secondary. Yet Benjamin insists that the model of their derivation is not that of resemblance or of imitation. It is not a natural process: the translation does not resemble the original the way the child resembles the parent, nor is it an imitation, a copy, or a paraphrase of the original. In that sense, since they are not resemblances, since they are not imitations, one would be tempted to say they are not metaphors. The translation is not the metaphor of the original; nevertheless, the German word for translation, *übersetzen*, means metaphor. *Übersetzen* translates exactly the Greek *metaphorein*, to move over, *übersetzen*, to put across. *Übersetzen*, I should say, *translates* metaphor — which, asserts Benjamin, is not at all the same. They are not metaphors, yet the word means metaphor. The metaphor is not a metaphor, Benjamin is saying. No wonder that translators have difficulty. It is a curious assumption to say *übersetzen* is not metaphorical, *übersetzen* is not based on resemblance, there is no resemblance between the translation and the original. Amazingly paradoxical statement, metaphor is not metaphor.

All these activities — critical philosophy, literary theory, history — resemble each other in the fact that they do not resemble that from which they derive. But they are all intralinguistic: they relate to what in the original belongs to language, and not to meaning as an extralinguistic correlate susceptible of paraphrase and imitation. They disarticulate, they undo the original, they reveal that the original was always already disarticulated. They reveal that their failure, which seems to be due to the fact that they are secondary in relation to the original, reveals an essential failure, an essential disarticulation which was already there in the original. They kill the original, by discovering that the original was already dead. They read the original from the perspective of a pure language (*reine Sprache*), a language that would be entirely freed of the illusion of meaning — pure form if you want; and in doing so they bring to light a dismembrance, a de-canonization which was already there in the original from the beginning. In the process of translation, as Benjamin understands it — which has little to do with the empirical act of translating, as all of us practice it on a daily basis — there is an inherent and particularly threatening danger. The emblem of that danger is Hölderlin's translations of Sophocles:

> Confirmation of this as well as of every other important aspect is supplied by Hölderlin's translations, particularly those of the two tragedies by Sophocles. In them the harmony of the languages is so profound that sense is touched by language only the way an aeolian harp is touched by the wind. . . Hölderlin's translations in particular are subject to the enormous danger inherent in all translations: the gates of a language thus expanded and modified may slam shut and enclose the translator with silence. Hölderlin's translations from Sophocles were his last work, in them meaning plunges from abyss to abyss until it threatens to become lost in the bottomless depths of language. (pp. 81-82)

Translation, to the extent that it disarticulates the original, to the extent that it is pure language and is only concerned with language, gets drawn into what he calls the bottomless depth, something essentially destructive, which is in language itself.

What translation does, by reference to the fiction or hypothesis of a pure language devoid of the burden of meaning, is that it implies — in bringing to light what Benjamin calls "die Wehen des eigenen" — the suffering of what one thinks of as one's own — the suffering of the original language. We think we are at ease in our own language, we feel a coziness, a familiarity, a shelter in the language we call our own, in which we think that we are not alienated. What the translation reveals is that this alienation is at its strongest in our relation to our own original language, that the original language within which we are engaged is disarticulated in a way which imposes upon us a particular alienation, a particular suffering. Here too the translators, with considerable unanimity, cannot see this statement. Benjamin's text is: "dass gerade unter allen Formen ihr also Eigenstes es zufällt, auf jene Nachreife des fremden Wortes, auf die Wehen des eigenen zu merken" (p. 54). The two translators — I guess they didn't correspond with each other, they did this d'un commun accord — translate Wehen, pains, as "birth pangs," as being particularly the pains of childbirth. Gandillac is very explicit about it, he calls it "les douleurs obstétricales" (p. 266) in the most literal, clinical way; Zohn says "birth pangs" (p. 73). Why they do this is a mystery. Wehen can mean birth pangs, but it does mean any kind of suffering, without necessarily the connotation of birth and rebirth, of resurrection, which would be associated with the notion of birth pangs because you suffer in producing something — and this is a magnificent moment, you'd be willing to suffer (especially easy for us to say). Benjamin has just been speaking of the "Nachreife des fremden Wortes," translated by Zohn as "maturing process," which again is wrong. Nachreife is like the German word Spätlese (a particularly good wine made from the late, rotten grape), it is like Stifter's novel Nachsommer ("Indian Summer") — it has the melancholy, the feeling of slight exhaustion, of life to which you are not entitled, happiness to which you are not entitled, time has passed, and so on. It is associated with another word that Benjamin constantly uses, the word überleben, to live beyond your own death in a sense. The translation belongs not to the life of the original, the original is already dead, but the translation belongs to the afterlife of the original, thus assuming and confirming the death of the original. Nachreife is of the same order, or has to do with the same; it is by no means a maturing process, it is a looking back on a process of maturity that is finished, and that is no longer taking place. So if you translate Wehen by "birth pangs," you would have to translate it by "death pangs" as much as by "birth pangs," and the stress is perhaps more on death than on life.

The process of translation, if we can call it a process, is one of change and of motion that has the appearance of life, but of life as an afterlife, because translation also reveals the death of the original. Why is this? What are those death pangs, possibly birth pangs, of the original? It is easy to say to some extent what this suffering is not. It is certainly not subjective pains, some kind of pathos of a self, a kind of manifestation of a self-pathos which the poet would have expressed as his sufferings. This is certainly not the case, because, says Benjamin, the sufferings that are here being mentioned are not in any sense human. They would certainly not be the sufferings of an individual, or of a subject. That also is very hard to see, for the translators. Zohn, confronted with that passage (I will stop this game of showing up the translators, but it is always of some interest), translates: "If they are referred exclusively to man" (p. 70). Benjamin very clearly says: "Wenn sie nicht . . . auf den Menschen bezogen werden" (p. 51), if you do not relate them to man. The stress is precisely that the suffering that is mentioned, the failure, is not a human failure; it does not refer therefore to any subjective experience. The original is unambiguous in that respect. This suffering is also not a kind of historical pathos, the pathos you heard in Hartman's reference to Benjamin as the one who had discovered the pathos of history; it is not this pathos of remembrance, or this pathetic mixture of hope and catastrophe and apocalypse which Hartman captures, which is present certainly in Benjamin's tone, but not so much in what he says. It is not the pathos of a history, it is not the pathos of what in Hölderlin is called the "dürftiger Zeit" between the disappearance of the gods and the possible return of the gods. It is not this kind of sacrificial, dialectical, and elegiac gesture, by means of which one looks back on the past as a period that is lost, which then gives you the hope of another future that may occur.

The reasons for this pathos, for this *Wehen*, for this suffering, are specifically linguistic. They are stated by Benjamin with considerable linguistic structural precision; so much so that if you come to a word like "abyss" in the passage about Hölderlin, where it is said that Hölderlin tumbles in the abyss of language, you should understand the word "abyss" in the non-pathetic, technical sense in which we speak of a *mise en abyme* structure, the kind of structure by means of which it is clear that the text becomes itself an example of what it exemplifies. The text about translation is itself a translation, and the untranslatability which it mentions about itself inhabits its own texture and will inhabit anybody who in his turn will try to translate it, as I am now trying, and failing, to do. The text is untranslatable: it was untranslatable for the translators who tried to do it, it is untranslatable for the commentators who talk about it, it is an example of what it states, it is a *mise en abyme* in the technical sense, a story within the story of what is its own statement.

What are the linguistic reasons which allow Benjamin to speak of a suffering, of a disarticulation, of a falling apart of any original work, or of any work to the extent that that work is a work of language? On this Benjamin is very precise, and offers us what amounts in very few lines to an inclusive theory of language. The disjunction is first of all between what he calls "das Gemeinte," what is meant, and the "Art des Meinens," the way in which language means; between logos and lexis, if you want — what a certain statement means, and the way in which the statement is meant to mean. Here the difficulties of the translators are a little more interesting, because they involve philosophical concepts that are of some importance. Gandillac, a philosopher who knows phenomenology and who writes in a period when phenomenology is the overriding philosophical pressure in France, translates by "visée intentionelle" (p. 272). The way we would now translate in French "das Gemeinte" and "Art des Meinens" would be by the distinction between *vouloir dire* and *dire*: "to mean," "to say." Zohn translates by "the intended object" and the "mode of intention" (p. 74). There is a phenomenological assumption here, and Gandillac has a footnote which refers to Husserl: both assume that the meaning and the way in which meaning is produced are intentional acts. But the problem is precisely that, whereas the meaning-function is certainly intentional, it is not *a priori* certain at all that the mode of meaning, the way in which I mean, is intentional in any way. The way in which I can try to mean is dependent upon linguistic properties that are not only [not] made by me, because I depend on the language as it exists for the devices which I will be using, it is as such not made by us as historical beings, it is perhaps not even made by humans at all. Benjamin says, from the beginning, that it is not at all certain that language is in any sense human. To equate language with humanity — as Schiller did — is in question. If language is not necessarily human — if we obey the law, if we function within language, and purely in terms of language — there can be no intent; there may be an intent of meaning, but there is no intent in the purely formal way in which we will use language independently of the sense or the meaning. The translation, which puts intentionality on both sides, both in the act of meaning and in the way in which one means, misses a philosophically interesting point — for what is at stake is the possibility of a phenomenology of language, or of poetic language, the possibility of establishing a poetics which would in any sense be a phenomenology of language.

How are we to understand this discrepancy between "das Gemeinte" and "Art des Meinens," between *dire* and *vouloir-dire*? Benjamin's example is the German word *Brot* and the French word *pain*. To mean "bread," when I need to name bread, I have the word *Brot*, so that the way in which I mean is by using the word *Brot*. The translation will reveal a fundamental discrepancy between the intent to name *Brot* and the word *Brot* itself in its materiality, as a device of meaning. If you hear *Brot* in this context of Hölderlin, who is so often mentioned in this text, I hear *Brot und Wein* necessarily, which is the great Hölderlin text that is very much present in this — which in French becomes *Pain et vin*. "Pain et vin" is what you get for free in a restaurant, in a cheap restaurant where it is still included, so *pain et vin* has very different connotations from *Brot und Wein*. It brings to mind the *pain français, baguette, ficelle, bâtard*, all those things — I now hear in *Brot* "bastard." This upsets the stability of the quotidian. I was very happy with the word *Brot*, which I hear as a native because my native language is Flemish and you say *brood*, just like in German, but if I have to think that *Brot [brood]* and *pain* are the same thing, I get very upset. It is all right in English because "bread" is close enough to *Brot [brood]*, despite the idiom "bread" for money, which has its problems. But the stability of my quotidian, of my daily bread, the reassuring quotidian aspects of the word "bread," daily bread, is upset by the French word *pain*. What I mean is upset by the way in which I mean — the way in which it is *pain,* the phoneme, the term *pain*, which has its set of connotations which take you in a completely different direction.

This disjunction is best understood (to take it to a more familiar theoretical problem) in terms of the difficult relationship between the hermeneutics and the poetics of literature. When you do hermeneutics, you are concerned with the meaning of the work; when you do poetics, you are concerned with the stylistics or with the description of the way in which a work means. The question is whether these two are complementary, whether you can cover the full work by doing hermeneutics and poetics at the same time. The experience of trying to do this shows that it is not the case. When one tries to achieve this complementarity, the poetics always drops out, and what one always does is hermeneutics. One is so attracted by problems of meaning that it is impossible to do hermeneutics and poetics at the same time. From the moment you start to get involved with problems of meaning, as I unfortunately tend to do, forget about the poetics. The two are not complementary, the two may be mutually exclusive in a certain way, and that is part of the problem which Benjamin states, a purely linguistic problem.

He states a further version of this when he speaks of a disjunction between the word and the sentence, *Wort* and *Satz*. *Satz* in German means not just sentence, in the grammatical sense, it means statement — Heidegger will speak of *Der Satz des Grundes*; *Satz* is the statement, the most fundamental statement, meaning — the most meaningful word — whereas word is associated by Benjamin with *Aussage*, the way in which you state, as the apparent agent of the statement. *Wort* means not only the agent of the statement as a lexical unit, but also as syntax and as grammar: if you look at a sentence in terms of words, you look at it not just in terms of particular words but also in terms of the grammatical relationships between those words. So the question of the relationship between word and sentence becomes, for Benjamin, the question of the compatibility between grammar and meaning. What is being put in question is precisely that compatibility, which we take for granted in a whole series of linguistic investigations. Are grammar (word and syntax), on the one hand, and meaning (as it culminates in the *Satz*), on the other hand — are they compatible with each other? Does the one lead to the other, does the one support the other? Benjamin tells us that translation puts that conviction in question because, he says, from the moment that a translation is really literal, *wörtlich*, word by word, the meaning completely disappears. The example is again Hölderlin's translations of Sophocles, which are absolutely literal, word by word, and which are therefore totally unintelligible; what comes out is completely incomprehensible, completely undoes the sentence, the *Satz* of Sophocles, which is entirely gone. The meaning of the word slips away (as we saw, a word like *Aufgabe*, which means task, also means something completely different, so that the word escapes us), and there is no grammatical way to control this slippage. There is also a complete slippage of the meaning when the translator follows the syntax, when he writes literally, *wörtlich*. And to some extent, a translator has to be *wörtlich*, has to be literal. The problem is best compared to the relationship between the letter and the word; the relationship between word and sentence is like the relationship between letter and word, namely, the letter is without meaning in relation to the word, it is *a-sēmos*, it is without meaning. When you spell a word you say a certain number of meaningless letters, which then come together in the word, but in each of the letters the word is not present. The two are absolutely independent of each other. What is being named here as the disjunction between grammar and meaning, *Wort* and *Satz*, is the materiality of the letter, the independence, or the way in which the letter can disrupt the ostensibly stable meaning of a sentence and introduce in it a slippage by means of which that meaning disappears, evanesces, and by means of which all control over that meaning is lost.

So we have, first, a disjunction in language between the hermeneutic and the poetic, we have a second one between grammar and meaning, and, finally, we will have a disjunction, says Benjamin, between the symbol and what is being symbolized, a disjunction on the level of tropes between the trope as such and the meaning as a totalizing power of tropological substitutions. There is a similar and equally radical disjunction, between what tropes (which always imply totalization) convey in terms of totalization and what the tropes accomplish taken by themselves. That seems to be the main difficulty of this particular text, because the text is full of tropes, and it selects tropes which convey the illusion of totality. It seems to relapse into the tropological errors that it denounces. The text constantly uses images of seed, of ripening, of harmony, it uses the image of seed and rind (*l'écorce et le noyau*) — which seem to be derived from analogies between nature and language, whereas the claim is constantly being made that there are no such analogies. In the same way that history is not to be understood in terms of an analogy with nature, tropes should not be based on resemblances with nature. But that is precisely the difficulty and the challenge of this particular text. Whenever Benjamin uses a trope which seems to convey a picture of total meaning, of complete adequacy between figure and meaning, a figure of perfect synecdoche in which the partial trope expresses the totality of a meaning, he manipulates the allusive context within his work in such a way that the traditional symbol is displaced in a manner that acts out the discrepancy between symbol and meaning, rather than the acquiescence between both.

One striking example of that is the image of the amphora:

Fragments of a vessel which are to be glued together must match one another in the smallest details, although they need not be like one another. In the same way, a translation, instead of resembling the meaning of the original, must lovingly and in detail incorporate the original's mode of signification, thus making both the original and the translation recognizable as fragments of a greater language, just as fragments are part of a vessel. For this very reason translation must in large measure refrain from wanting to communicate . . . (p. 78).

According to this image, there is an original, pure language, of which any particular work is only a fragment. That would be fine, provided we could, through that fragment, find access again to the original work. The image is that of a vessel, of which the literary work would be a piece, and then the translation is a piece of that. It is admitted that the translation is a fragment; but if the translation relates to the original as a fragment relates, if the translation would reconstitute as such the original, then — although it does not resemble it, but matches it perfectly (as in the word *symbolon*, which states the matching of two pieces or two fragments) — then we can think of any particular work as being a fragment of the pure language, and then indeed Benjamin's statement would be a religious statement about the fundamental unity of language.

Benjamin has told us, however, that the symbol and what it symbolizes, the trope and what it seems to represent, do not correspond. How is this to be made compatible with a statement like the one made here? An article by Carol Jacobs called "The Monstrosity of Translation," which appeared in *Modern Language Notes*, treats this passage in a way which strikes me as exceedingly precise and correct. First, she is aware of the Kabbalistic meaning of the text, by referring to Gershom Scholem, who in writing about this text relates the figure of the angel to the history of the *Tikkun* of the Lurianic Kabbalah:

> Yet at the same time Benjamin has in mind the Kabbalistic concept of the *Tikkun*, the messianic restoration and mending which patches together and restores the original Being of things, shattered and corrupted in the "Breaking of Vessels," and also [the original being of] history.

Carol Jacobs comments:

> Scholem might have turned to "Die Aufgabe des Übersetzers," where the image of the broken vessel plays a more direct role. . . . Yet whereas Zohn suggests that a totality of fragments are brought together, Benjamin insists that the final outcome is still "a broken part."[5]

All you have to do, to see that, is translate correctly, instead of translating like Zohn — who made this difficult passage very clear — but who in the process of making it clear made it say something completely different. Zohn said, "fragments of a vessel which are to be glued together must match one another in the smallest detail." Benjamin said, translated by Carol Jacobs word by word, "fragments of a vessel, in order to be *articulated* together" — which is much better than *glued* together, which has a totally irrelevant concreteness — "must *follow* one another in the smallest detail" — which is not at all the same as *match* one another. What is already present in this difference is that we have *folgen*, not *gleichen*, not to match. We have a metonymic, a successive pattern, in which things follow, rather than a metaphorical unifying pattern in which things become one by resemblance. They do not match each other, they follow each other; they are already metonyms and not metaphors; as such they are certainly less working toward a convincing tropological totalization than if we use the term "match." But things get more involved, or more distorted, in what follows.

So, instead of making itself similar to the meaning, to the *Sinn* of the original, the translation must rather, lovingly and in detail, in its own language, form itself according to the manner of meaning [*Art des Meinens*] of the original, to make both recognizable as the broken parts of the greater language, just as fragments are the broken parts of a vessel.

That is entirely different from saying, as Zohn says:

in the same way a translation, instead of resembling the meaning of the original, must lovingly and in detail incorporate the original's mode of signification, thus making both the original and the translation recognizable as fragments of a greater language, just as fragments are part of a vessel.

"Just as fragments are part of a vessel" is a synecdoche; "just as fragments," says Benjamin, "are the *broken* parts of a vessel"; as such he is not saying that the fragments constitute a totality, he says the fragments are fragments, and that they remain essentially fragmentary. They follow each other up, metonymically, and they will never constitute a totality. I'm reminded of an example I heard given by the French philosopher Michel Serres — that you find out about fragments by doing the dishes: if you break a dish it breaks into fragments, but you can't break the fragments any more. That's an optimistic, a positive synecdochal view of the problem of fragments, because there the fragments can make up a whole, and you cannot break up the fragments. What we have here is an initial fragmentation; any work is totally fragmented in relation to this *reine Sprache*, with which it has nothing in common, and every translation is totally fragmented in relation to the original. The translation is the fragment of a fragment, is breaking the fragment — so the vessel keeps breaking, constantly — and never reconstitutes it; there was no vessel in the first place, or we have no knowledge of this vessel, or no awareness, no access to it, so for all intents and purposes there has never been one.

Therefore the distinction between symbol and symbolized, the nonadequation of symbol to a shattered symbolized, the nonsymbolic character of this adequation, is a version of the others, and indicates the unreliability of rhetoric as a system of tropes which would be productive of a meaning. Meaning is always displaced with regard to the meaning it ideally intended — that meaning is never reached. Benjamin approaches the question in terms of the aporia between freedom and faithfulness, the question which haunts the problem of translation. Does translation have to be faithful, or does it have to be free? For the sake of the idiomatic relevance of the target language, it has to be free; on the other hand, it has to be faithful, to some extent, to the original. The faithful translation, which is always literal, how can it also be free? It can only be free if it reveals the instability of the original, and if it reveals that instability as the linguistic tension between trope and meaning. Pure language is perhaps more present in the translation than in the original, but in the mode of trope. Benjamin, who is talking about the inability of trope to be adequate to meaning, constantly uses the very tropes which seem to postulate the adequation between meaning and trope; but he prevents them in a way, displaces them in such a way as to put the original in motion, to de-canonize the original, giving it a movement which is a movement of disintegration, of fragmentation. This movement of the original is a wandering, an *errance*, a kind of permanent exile if you wish, but it is not really an exile, for there is no homeland, nothing from which one has been exiled. Least of all is there something like a *reine Sprache*, a pure language, which does not exist except as a permanent disjunction which inhabits all languages as such, including and especially the language one calls one's own. What is to be one's own language is the most displaced, the most alienated of all.

Now it is this motion, this errancy of language which never reaches the mark, which is always displaced in relation to what it meant to reach, it is this errancy of language, this illusion of a life that is only an afterlife, that Benjamin calls history. As such, history is not human, because it pertains strictly to the order of language; it is not natural, for the same reason; it is not phenomenal, in the sense that no cognition, no knowledge about man, can be derived from a history which as such is purely a linguistic complication; and it is not really temporal either, because the structure that animates it is not a temporal structure. Those disjunctions in language do get expressed by temporal metaphors, but they are only metaphors. The dimension of futurity, for example, which is present in it, is not temporal but is the correlative of the figural pattern and the disjunctive power which Benjamin locates in the structure of language. History, as Benjamin conceives it, is certainly not messianic, since it consists in the rigorous separation and the acting out of the separation of the sacred from the poetic, the separation of the *reine Sprache* from poetic language. *Reine Sprache*, the sacred language, has nothing in common with poetic language; poetic language does not resemble it, poetic language does not depend on it, poetic language has nothing to do with it. It is within this negative knowledge of its relation to the language of the sacred that poetic language initiates. It is, if you want, a necessarily nihilistic moment that is necessary in any understanding of history.

Benjamin said this in the clearest of terms, not in this essay but in another text called "Theological and Political Fragment,"[6] from which I will quote a short passage in conclusion. He said it with all possible clarity, it seemed to me, until I tried to translate that particular passage, and found that English happens to have a property which makes it impossible to translate. Here is the passage:

Only the messiah himself puts an end to history, in the sense that it frees, completely fulfills the relationship of history to the messianic. Therefore, nothing that is truly historical can want to relate by its own volition to the messianic. Therefore the kingdom of God is not the telos of the dynamics of history, it cannot be posited as its aim; seen historically it is not its aim but its end.

That is where I have a great deal of trouble with English, because the English word for "aim" can also be "end." You say "the end and the means," the aim and the means by which you achieve it. And the English word "end" can mean just as well *Ziel* as it can mean *Ende*. My end, my intention. So that if we want to use that idiom, the translation then becomes: "seen historically it is not its end but its end," its termination — it would be perfect English. But it would indicate that the separation which is here undertaken by Benjamin is hidden in this word "end" in English, which substitutes for "aim" the word "end," the two things which Benjamin asks us to keep rigorously apart.

It cannot be posited as its aim; seen historically it is not its aim but its end, its termination; therefore the order of the profane cannot be constructed in terms of the idea of the sacred. Therefore theocracy does not have a political but only a religious meaning.

And Benjamin adds:

To have denied the political significance of theocracy, to have denied the political significance of the religious, messianic view, to have denied this with all desirable intensity is the great merit of Bloch's book *The Spirit of Utopia*.

Since we saw that what is here called political and historical is due to purely linguistic reasons, we can in this passage replace "political" by "poetical," in the sense of a poetics. For we now see that the nonmessianic, nonsacred, that is the *political* aspect of history is the result of the *poetical* structure of language, so that political and poetical here are substituted, in opposition to the notion of the sacred. To the extent that such a poetics, such a history, is nonmessianic, not a theocracy but a rhetoric, it has no room for certain historical notions such as the notion of modernity, which is always a dialectical, that is to say an essentially theological notion. You will remember that we started out from Gadamer's claim to modernity, in terms of a dialectic which was explicitly associated with the word "Spirit," with the spirituality in the text of Hegel. We have seen, and it is for me gratifying to find, that Hegel himself — when, in the section of the *Aesthetics* on the sublime, he roots the sublime in this same separation between sacred and profane — is actually much closer to Benjamin in "The Task of the Translator" than he is to Gadamer.

Questions

de Man: I'll be glad to take questions of a more general nature. If there are questions you want to bring up that pertain not just to Benjamin but to other problems that have been raised, I'll be happy to try to answer them . . . . I have deliberately . . . Yes?

Billy Flesch: Is it necessary to see intention as subjective . . .

de Man: No.

Flesch: . . . or can you have intention, can you get rid of the subject without being left only with language?

de Man: Well, intention is not seen here as necessarily subjective, but it is seen as necessarily semantic. Intention is inseparable from the concept of meaning; any meaning is to some extent intentional. Any language oriented to meaning is at least intentional, precisely by virtue of the fact that it intends meaning. Intention is, therefore, not subjective. Intention in Husserl, in phenomenology as it establishes itself as a serious philosophical discipline, is not simply subjective, it is rather primarily a critique of the notion of the subject as simply the expression of its own wishfulness, or something of the sort. But intentionality always has a semantic function; intentionality is always directed toward a meaning, toward the explicit meaning — that is always intentional. It is always a *visée*, Gandillac's translation is correct in speaking of a *visée intentionelle* — the language aims at, sets itself as the target, the meaning which it sets. As such, it is not subjective, but it is semantically determined — semantically rather than semiotically, if you want — as it would be in a poetics as opposed to a hermeneutics. A hermeneutics is always intentional, to the extent that it is a description of technical devices which exist independently of the meaning at which they aim, and are not determined by the intentional gesture in any sense. Yes? I'll get to you in a second.

Neil Hertz: I want to pick up on the relation between the transpersonal and the inhuman.

de Man: Right.

Hertz: Because it seems that — I'm talking about the moment when you were talking about poetry — and *Brot* — and *pain* — . . .

de Man: Right, uh huh.

Hertz: When you give that as an instance, you tend to adduce the kinds of connotations that words develop over a long time and historical culture, so that their quotidian feel, for you, is in some relation to the fact that Hölderlin wrote a poem, and that Christians do certain things with bread, and so forth and so on. Now, all of those instances add up to what's beyond your control as an individual user of language, but they don't quite add up to the inhuman.

de Man: No.

Hertz: And it's that movement that I want — there's a mediation in there someplace.

de Man: Right, well . . .

Hertz: Now suppose you put this in connection with the mathematical sublime — imagine that the totality that you are trying to apprehend, or comprehend, I forget which of those terms is what you can't do and which one you can do —

de Man: You can apprehend, to a certain point, but after a certain point you can't comprehend what you apprehend.

Hertz: Imagine a sequence of apprehensions about the meaning of *Brot*. You take in Hölderlin, you take in a whole series of other German ones, you take in the Christian connotation and so forth and so on; similarly you've got a series of apprehensions about *pain*, that goes off in its own direction. It's conceivable that the moment when the word "inhuman" comes to mind is the moment of the breakdown of those acts of apprehension. That's very prosaic. I mean it's because there are a whole series of events, in what we ordinarily call history, that lose connotations, and they get lost, one loses track of them; and we name some of them, one poem by Hölderlin, we can't name others, and so forth and so on. It seems to me that you want to hold on to the prosaic nature of the inhuman —

de Man: Right.

Hertz: — because that's an important word in your own discourse.

de Man: Right.

Hertz: At the same time, the word "inhuman" keeps pulling in the direction of the mysterious. You no? [laughter] Not for you? Maybe it doesn't. Not in a mode of terror, but just in a mode of the substantiation and the individuation of something that's *the* Inhuman, like *the* Sublime . . .

de Man: Yah.

Hertz: It's become a singular noun, covering a series of failed apprehensions.

de Man: Yah.

Hertz: It's that transition I'm puzzled by, how you get from what's really a contingent impossibility — to reconstruct the connotations of *Brot* — to a major term, like the "Inhuman."

de Man: Well, you're quite right. I was indulging myself, you know, it was long, and I was very aware of potential boredom, felt the need for an anecdote, for some relief, and Benjamin gives the example of *pain* and *Brot*, and perhaps shouldn't . . . whenever you give an example you, as you know, lose what you want to say; and Benjamin, by giving the example of *pain* and *Brot* — which comes from him — and which I've banalized, for the sake of a cheap laugh. . . . Well, as you say, it went from a problem of apprehension, comprehension — which is a simple tropological problem — you come to the inhuman, which Benjamin mentions in a somewhat different context from that of *pain* and *Brot* — I should not have quoted that — but that is still very human, what happens there. The ''inhuman,'' however, is not some kind of mystery, or some kind of secret; the inhuman is: linguistic structures, the play of linguistic tensions, linguistic events that occur, possibilities which are inherent in language — independently of any intent or any drive or any wish or any desire we might have. So that, more than nature, toward which one can have, toward which one sets up, a human rapport — which is illegitimate, as illegitimate as turns out to be, in the final run, the interpersonal rapport, which is illegitimate too, since there is, in a very radical sense, no such thing as the human. If one speaks of the inhuman, the fundamental non-human character of language, one also speaks of the fundamental non-definition of the human as such, since the word human doesn't correspond to anything like that. So by extension, any . . . but let's not go that far — I'm now ahead of the statement . . . . What in language does not pertain to the human, what in language is unlike nature and is not assimilable, or doesn't resemble, what in language does not resemble the human in any way, is totally indifferent in relation to the human, is not therefore mysterious; it is eminently prosaic, and what happens — what is precisely interesting, I think — is that Benjamin's language of pathos, language of historical pathos, language of the messianic, the pathos of exile and so on and so forth, really describes linguistic events which are by no means human. So that what he calls the pains of the original become structural deficiencies which are best analyzed in terms of the inhuman, dehumanized language of linguistics, rather than into the language of imagery, or tropes, of pathos, or drama, which he chooses to use in a very peculiar way. To the extent that this text is human, all too human in the appeal it makes to you, and its messianic overtones to name something which is essentially nonhuman, it displaces our sense of what is human, both in ourselves and in our relationship to other humans. In a very fundamental way, I think. So that, from the statement that language is not human, that history is not human, which is made at the beginning, we are now brought to see something about the human which goes beyond that in that sense . . . whether it is mysterious, whether that is inhuman, or whether that is . . . the sacred, or something, one is impelled to read *reine Sprache* as that which is the most sacred, which is the most divine, when in fact in Benjamin it means a language completely devoid of any kind of meaning function, language which would be pure signifier, which would be completely devoid of any semantic function whatsoever, a purely technical linguistic language — and it would be purely limited to its own linguistic characteristics. You can call that divine or sacred, if you want, but it is not mysterious in that sense, I think, though it is paradoxical in the extreme. . . .

Unidentified: I'm a little concerned about what became of the original. In the way that you handled it, you talked about the destabilization of the original, and that translation goes beyond the original. There's a problem for me, because what happens to the original, if the original becomes nonexistent? [. . .] I don't know what to do with it. I understand what you were doing, but I don't understand what happens in terms of the original, at least in terms of, let's say, pragmatic usage.

de Man: Well, that would precisely be what is impossible. This is irreversibility again, we have here an example of irreversibility, to the extent that you could not possibly get from the translation back to an original. Somebody who would have a translation and — well yesterday I was reading a piece of ordinary professional prose, I was translating with some discomfort Mrs. Wilkinson's text,[7] which is written in English, but I happen to have only a German translation, so I translated — I certainly didn't get the original. Whatever I have produced there — this piece of Wilkinson's, which still I give the name of Wilkinson, would perhaps be, would relate to the original in a very interesting way, which would raise some questions about the nature of what she had originally said there. I certainly have stressed things which I want to see, that she didn't want to see, and so on, so that that text is destabilized by that. What happens to the original? First of all Benjamin says: take the notion of *Fortleben*, of survival, in the most literal sense possible, take it as literally as you can take it, it is the survival of the text, the text is kept in circulation, by the translation, circulation is augmented as such in the process. But what happens to the original, which is your question — there are many words for it, it is decanonized, it is — you are made aware of certain disjunctions, certain disruptions, certain accommodations, certain weaknesses, certain cheatings, certain conventions, certain characteristics which don't correspond to the *claim* of the original, so that the original loses its sacred character — of being the original in any sense — one of the sacred characters it loses is that of its claim of originality, because a translation brings out all that is idiomatical, all that is customary, all that is quotidian, all that is nonsacred, all that is *prosaic* in the original — translation is a prosaization of the original, always, to a considerable extent. [. . .] The translation is a making prosaic of what *appeared* to be poetic in the original. As such, the translation is a prosaization; therefore the translation is a slave, as Hegel said, the prosaic slave, and so on, of the original. And what happens to the original—I think can be said—the original is disarticulated, the original is reduced to the status of prose, is decanonized, all that by the process of translation, because the impossibility of translation is due to disruptions which *are* there in the original, but which the original managed to hide — in the same way that Benjamin manages to hide, from the reader, from the translator, from everybody who reads this text, manages to hide, for example, the inadequacy of any symbol in relation to what it means, by using symbols which are particularly convincing, which are particularly seductive, and which seem precisely to achieve what they want to achieve, what they mean to achieve. He does it, and as such he produces an original text which has the beauty and seduction of an original text, and generally Benjamin gets praised for the magnificence of his images, and so on and so forth; but they are quite perverse in the way in which they undo the claim that is associated with them. The translation is a way of reading the original which will reveal those inherent weaknesses in the original, not in the sense that the original is then no longer a great work or anything, or that it wouldn't be worthy of admiration or anything of the sort, but in a much more fundamental way: that the original is not canonical, that the original is a piece of ordinary language, in a way — prosaic, ordinary language — which as such belongs as much to that category as [to the category of original]. It is desacralized. De-canonized, desacralized, in a very fundamental way. If you then think of the original as being Dante or Pindar, and you put that next to the way in which those authors are constantly sacralized — then you started from the notion of George, as the one who sacralizes the notion of the poet — then you would see, in a sense, what happens to the original. Yes?

Richard Klein: I just want to go back to what Neil was saying about the Inhuman. I wonder if there would be some inhumanness that one could attach for example to the problems of translation, say, if from *ode* to *tableau*, there would be an inhumanity that wouldn't belong to the nature of the mathematical sublime, let's say wouldn't have to do with the inexhaustible, infinite connotations inherent in language, making it impossible ever to stop the process of translation, but that would be a kind of . . . which would imply a sort of abyss if you like, to get back to that term — but the sort of specular abyss like when you see a mirror in a mirror, the images keep on getting smaller and smaller. But this would be that other kind of abyss that you mentioned, where the relationship would be the terms that are being translated to one another, have that kind of a negative synecdochal relationship of a part which is a part of a whole of which it is not a part — somehow more than a whole, and that would emblematize in the inhuman way which the translations of Benjamin were constantly founding their own inhumanity, requiring their position as parts of what they were . . .

de Man: Well, I see. In a way, what Gandillac, and Zohn too — very nice gentlemen, especially Zohn, who's very nice — Gandillac a little less — but at least they're human! — what they did to Benjamin is inhuman! It's inhuman not to see that *nicht* is there, that's not human. Humanely, you would see that; but it's not mechanical either, it's just inhuman! I don't know what to say — *ça ne se fait pas*, it's scandalous! It's scandalous in that sense, right? It would indeed be . . indeed along *these* lines. "Inhuman" becomes a curious and all-invading concept here. Well, it's a little bit qualified in that Benjamin — because , . . . well, let's not go into that, this notion of the inhuman. Mike?

Meyer Abrams: I want to go back to the question that Neil, Professor Neil Hertz, raised about language being somehow opposed to the human. And the grounds on which one makes such a claim. I want to do what I did yesterday . . .

de Man: Sure.

Abrams: . . . not to oppose your claim, not even to complement it, but simply to provide a different perspective, just so we can settle the matter in another way. And that perspective won't surprise you because you've heard it before and expect it from me.

de Man: That's very human.

Abrams: Suppose I should say, as many people have said before me, that instead of being the nonhuman, language is the most human of all the things we find in the world, in that language is entirely the product of human beings. That syntax, tropes, and all the other operations of language, are equally human, since they are part of the language. Human beings develop a language system which involves regularities of some sort, on which we can play, otherwise language wouldn't be language — you would have a unique instance every time you said something. That would not only be nonsystemic, it would be nonsense. Now, suppose that, alternatively to looking at the play of grammar, syntax, trope, as somehow opposed to meaning, I should say — and I'm not alone in saying this — that language, through all these aspects, doesn't get between itself and the meaning — but instead that language, when used by people, makes its meanings. So that meanings are not something we can oppose to language, but are something that language, when used by people, means. Now in that case, both language and meaning become the intrinsically human, the most human of things. By such a criterion, I can say, as many people have indeed said: What can be more human than the language which distinguishes human beings from all other living things? You know the play of this dialectic.

de Man: Sure.

Abrams: So we end up with a scene in which language, which you say is something opposed to the human and opposed to meaning, is the most human of things, and *makes* its meanings, to which it cannot be opposed — unless you establish alternative criteria of meaning which make it opposable to what language in fact says. Now, it seems to me that in doing so you are making a move that falls into the trap of some of the people you oppose, in which somehow meaning exists independently of language as it tries to make meaning. Is there a paradox there? I'm not sure. But at any rate, all I want to do is present the humanistic perspective, as an alternative, an optional alternative, which appeals to me. Instinctively, it appeals to me.

de Man: Well, it appeals to me also, greatly; and there is no question of its appeal, and its desirability. There is no question that language means, and that language . . . Let's get back to our text. Benjamin is not talking of the ordinary use of language. He's not speaking of the quotidian use, or of the poetic as an extension — or a sublimation, or whatever you want to call it — in which one would think of poetic language as being just more meaning, more expressive, richer, more complex meaning than other — but always meaning. He is not speaking of the ordinary use of language. He's speaking of the very peculiar, unusual, and uncommon element in language called translation: something that language allows one to do, which is translation within language. Translation, which presupposes meaning, and which presupposes a circulation of meaning, whether it is within the same language, whether it is in — the way we are inter-changing language now, in the way I translate what you're saying, I can . . . so on and so forth — and he discovers a difficulty. There is a difficulty inherent in translation. And moreover, this seems to be the case, because the translators of his own text seem to run into similar difficulties. The suggestion is not that language doesn't mean; the suggestion is that there is a question about the semantic value of language. Desirable as it is, and indispensable as it is, of course — go back to Eisenhower and religion: "We must have language!" No, that is somewhere else . . . They asked Eisenhower what to do about religion, and he said, "We must have it!" The same is true about language as meaning: we must have it. Imagine that we didn't! Nobody is suggesting that we should do away with it. But there *is* a question, a question of language. Let's transpose it within the historical scheme which you bring up: the notion of the definition of man by his language. Man is the animal that speaks, is the speaking animal. There is that historical topos which comes back, and one thinks of Hamann, one thinks of some others, and it says — and that is to some extent Benjamin's concern here — "At the beginning was the word."[8] Language is not human, it is God-given: it is the logos, as that which God gives to man. Not specifically to man, but God gives, as such. That's not at all the same as to say man is man to the extent that he has language. And there is — well, I don't have to tell you — there is a constant danger between this notion of language as revealed trope — and as such not being human in any sense, something which man receives, as such, at a certain moment, and with which he has nothing to do — and the other notion of language as that which man has elaborated in a sense, as he goes about it pragmatically, justifying all those funny theories of language in the eighteenth century, where you argue whether they began with nouns or with verbs — this whole notion of language as natural process, versus language as divinely revealed. That it is divine or not makes little difference, and the more you take the sacred out of this picture, the better. But it indicates a constant problem about the nature of language as being either human or nonhuman. That there is a nonhuman aspect of language is a perennial awareness from which we cannot escape, because language does things which are so radically out of our control that they cannot be assimilated to the human at all, against which one fights constantly. So, I don't think that — the humanistic perspective is obviously there, there is no question that it has to be there — it is from the moment that a certain kind of critical examination — and that examination *has to* take place, it has to take place not out of some perversity, not out of some hubris of critical thought or anything of the sort, it has to take place because it addresses the question of what actually happens. Things happen in the world which cannot be accounted for in terms of the human conception of language. And they always happen in linguistic terms, or the relation [to] language is always involved when they have [happened]. And good or bad things, not only catastrophes, but felicities also. And they happen. In a sense, to account for them, to account for them historically, to account for them in any sense, a certain initial discrepancy in language has to be examined. You can't — it cannot be avoided. Philosophy has never been able to avoid the question of the proper nature . . . never, never, no matter in what way it presented itelf, however it presented itself as it inheres to language. Philosophy originates in this difficulty about the nature of language which is as such . . . and which is a difficulty about the definition of the human, or a difficulty within the human as such. And I think there is no escape from that.

Abrams: Let me indicate the extent to which I agree with you, very briefly. Of course translation is impossible, if you establish criteria for the exact translation from one language to another which makes translation unachievable. But one way of putting the matter is to say that each of the two is a different language, and that each language makes its own meanings. So I wouldn't oppose what Benjamin said, although some of the ways in which he gets at the matter puzzle me. Your second point I also agree with, but I would put it that what's wrong is not the operation of language but theories of language. It puzzles me that one tends, in making language problematic, to project upon language claims that seem to me rather to be applicable to theories of language. One such claim, for example, is that language deconstructs itself, when one seems actually to be claiming that no theory of language that anyone has ever proposed is unproblematic, so that all theories are self-deconstructive. And so while I could accept everything you've said, I would put it in this form: What's problematic is the theorization; language only becomes problematic when we theorize about it.

de Man: Yes, on the other hand . . .

Abrams: We use it. We may use it well or we may use it ill; we make it work, but sometimes it doesn't work — there's nothing inherently problematic about that.

de Man: Yes, but precisely — we can continue this, but just one more statement: theorization, the theorization of language, is initially and fundamentally a part of language. And I won't refer to what, in Benjamin — again, to bring it back to this particular text, and to the historical context of this particular text — the context of that is Friedrich Schlegel — this, a certain type of German Romanticism, which has . . . which Benjamin knows very well where it comes from, in which he has his allegiance — where precisely the necessary element of theorization in language, the fact that criticism — what is called by Friedrich Schlegel criticism — and poetry are inseparable. That there is no poetry without criticism of poetry, and that the two necessarily involve each other. I give this the merest name "theorization." The theorization is inherent in language. A language which would not be — and this has nothing to do with common and ordinary language: there's nothing more theoretical than the language on the street, than the common language which . . . The only people who believe that there is language that is not theoretical are professors of literature. They are the only ones who think . . . If you ask the people, they know that language is theoretical, that language is always, and that language is constantly — with the people, whoever that is. If you get popular uses of language, they are highly, infinitely theoretical, they are constantly metalinguistic, they constantly turn back upon language. Or if you see what mass manifestations of language, or mythologies are, they are always highly theorized. The notion of separating theory is a very understandable, nostalgic move in our profession, I'm afraid . . . I think so, I'm afraid.

Dominick LaCapra: It seems to me that, from what you're saying, it's not simply a question of a humanistic perspective, but that there is a sense in which, let's say, hermeneutics and poetics are compatible in the somewhat paradoxical sense that they have to suffer one another, in a rather strange way — in that sense metaphors of marriage might not be altogether out of place — but what struck me as really disconcerting in what you were saying, is that, on the left today, I think Benjamin is being introduced as someone who gives us all of the . . . all the subtlety of contemporary French criticism, with a political dimension that's very much identified with messianic hope and utopianism.

de Man: Right.

LaCapra: And from what you're arguing, I think that . . .

de Man: This is not just from what I'm arguing, this is on the basis of what Benjamin very openly and directly says. But when he says "ja," one understands "nein." And when he says "nein," one understands "ja." And that's very interesting: how this particular combination of Benjamin's political and critical powers, with some kind of affirmation of messianic futurity — that way madness lies. And that should be resisted, to some extent. Take that very simple statement: his approval of Bloch. Some reservations about Adorno, but the approval of Bloch's book on *The Spirit of Utopia*. Unreserved approval of it, of the book which argues absolutely against the messianic. It's much better. Because at least a nihilistic stance at that moment is possibly preparatory to a historical act. Whereas — and one would feel closer to Nietzsche there — Benjamin would be closer to certain elements in Nietzsche than he is to a messianic tradition which he spent his entire life holding at bay. The man who bears a strong responsibility in this unhappy misinterpretation of Benjamin is Scholem, who deliberately tried to make Benjamin say the opposite of what he said for ends of his own. But that has to do with . . . But the theme of the Frankfurt School interpretation of Benjamin is shot through with messianic elements which certainly are there, as a desire in Benjamin, but which Benjamin managed to control by an extraordinarily refined and deliberate strategy of both echoing themes, allowing them to enter his text, but then displacing them in his text in such a way that an attentive reading would reveal them. That attentive reading is very difficult to give. He succeeded so well in incorporating them in their displacement that you — it takes really a long practice — it's always lost again. Whenever I go back to this text, I think I have it more or less, then I read it again, and again I don't understand it. I again see a messianic appeal. There are many aspects of the text which I have not discussed, and which would in a sense, which would take work on my part to insert what I'm trying to say, especially at the end. The reason I haven't done it is not that . . . but there is a limit to time, but the end is . . . the interlinear commentary, you know, translation of Scripture, and so on. I would refer . . . well, to those who are interested in it, I refer again to Carol Jacobs's article, which does on that particular piece a very good job. Yes?

Tom Reinert: Can you elaborate on your notion of historical events? You referred to occurrences yesterday, in a way I found slightly obscure.

de Man: Occurrence. I suppose I've said that, used that a couple of times now — yesterday, too. In Benjamin, things don't seem to occur so much . . . there is a constant drifting, there is a constant (I said) *errance*, a constant . . . the movement is that of a constant displacement, of a constant exile, of a constant alienation in a sense, that persists. Actually, the text from which I quoted, the "Theologico-Political Fragment," ends up on the word "nihilism," and mentions nihilism as such. One could say, with all kinds of precautions, and in the right company, and with all kinds of reservations, that — and I think that's a very small company — that Benjamin's concept of history is nihilistic. Which would have to be understood as a very positive statement about it. In the same way that in Nietzsche nihilism is the necessary stage, and is accounted for in those terms. Understand by nihilism a certain kind of critical awareness which will not allow you to make certain affirmative statements when those affirmative statements go against the way things are. Therefore there is not in Benjamin, at this point, a statement about history as occurrence, as that which occurs, as events that occur. I think that what is implied, that what occurs, for example, is — translation is an occurrence. At the moment when translation really takes place, for example Hölderlin's translation of Sophocles, which undid Sophocles, undid Hölderlin, and revealed a great deal — that's an occurrence. That's an event, that is a historical event. As such, the occurrence can be textual, is generally textual, but it is an occurrence, in the sense that it is not . . . not . . . not the end of an error, but the recognition of the true nature of that error. He has described Hölderlin in his constant falling, and he says, "*Aber es gibt ein Halten.*" Which one tends to read as saying, "but there is a stop to this," one can stop this if you go to the sacred text. You can read it to mean, "*Aber es gibt ein Halten,*" in which you hold on to this obstinately, to this notion of *errance*, that you stay with it, in a sense. Then something occurs in the very act of your persisting in this, in this . . . that you don't give in to everything that would go in the other direction. At that moment, translation occurs. In Hölderlin, translation *occurs*. Most of the translations that are on the market are not translations in Benjamin's sense. When Luther translated, translated the Bible, something occurred — at that moment, something happened — not in the immediate sense that from then on there were wars and then the course of history was changed — that is a by-product. What really occurred was that . . . translation. Then there are, in the history of texts, texts which are occurrences. I think Rousseau's *Social Contract* is an occurrence, not because it is a political text, but something that occurs, in that sense. I realize this is difficult — a little obscure, and not well formulated. But I feel it, that there is something there. Something being said there which is kind of important to me, which I think . . . which isn't clear.

Notes

1. The German text, which appeared in *Aspekte der Modernität* (Göttingen: Vanderhoeck & Ruprecht, 1965), pp. 77-100, is most readily available in Gadamer's *Kleine Schriften* (Tübingen: J. C. B. Mohr, 1967), v. I, pp. 131-48. An English translation may be found in the collection *Philosophical Hermeneutics*, trans. David E. Linge, (Berkeley: University of California Press, 1976), pp. 107-29. cf. *Kleine Schriften*, v. I, p. 141; *Philosophical Hermeneutics*, p. 119.

2. Cf. *Kleine Schriften*, v, I, p. 141; *Philosophical Hermeneutics*, p. 128.

3. Walter Benjamin, "The Task of the Translator," in *Illuminations*, Harry Zohn, trans. (New York: Schocken Books, 1969), p. 69. Quotations from the French translation of Maurice de Gandillac are taken from Walter Benjamin, *Oeuvres* (Paris: Editions Denoël, 1971). Page numbers referring to either of these versions are given in parentheses; translations not identified with a page number are the author's. Page numbers supplied with quotations in German refer to the paperback *Illuminationen* (Frankfurt: Suhrkamp, 2d ed., 1980).

4. Geoffrey H. Hartman, *Criticism in the Wilderness: The Study of Literature Today* (New Haven: Yale University Press, 1980), p. 78.

5. Carol Jacobs, "The Monstrosity of Translation," *Modern Language Notes*, v. 90 (1975), p. 763, note 9.

6. Cf. *Illuminationen*, p. 262. An English translation of the "Theologico-Political Fragment" may be found in *Reflections*, Edmund Jephcott, trans., Peter Demetz, ed. (New York: Harcourt Brace Jovanovich, 1978), pp. 312-13.

7. Her introduction to Friedrich Schiller, *On the Aesthetic Education of Man*, Elizabeth M. Wilkinson and L.A. Willoughby, eds. and trans. (Oxford: Clarendon Press, 1967).

8. De Man's manuscript notes include a sheet on which he wrote only: "Im Anfang war das Wort und das Wort war bei Gott / Dasselbe war bei Gott / ohne Dasselbe" (the last two words lined out) — the beginning of Luther's translation of the Gospel according to John. Benjamin quotes the passage in Greek.

Dialogue and Dialogism

The set of problems that surrounds the general topic of this issue,[1] the relationship between fiction and reality in the novel, recurs in many forms to organize contemporary theories of narration as well as of the relationship between narrative, discursive and poetic language. Much is at stake, stylistically, philosophically, and historically, in these discussions whose importance, not only in the realm of theory but also in the practical sphere of ethics and politics, is superseded only by their difficulty. The higher the stakes the harder the game. Such situations, conducive to obsession and to fatigue, are prone to generate legitimate admiration with regard to predecessors who have somehow managed to sustain the ordeal of these difficulties and to bequeath to us some of the skills and strategies gained in the course of this experience. Literary theory, and especially theory of narrative, a rather barren area of endeavor constantly threatened by the tedium of its techniques as well as by the magnitude of the issues, offers poor soil for the heroes and the hero-worship that it rather desperately needs. So when a possible candidate for such a status comes along, he is likely to be very well received, especially if he is safely and posthumously out of reach. Such belated "receptions," for being rare, are all the more intense in the field of literary theory. A fairly recent example is, of course, the case of Walter Benjamin. More recent, and more intense still, is that of Mikhail Bakhtin, who was recently heralded, by his highly competent and clear-eyed introducers, as "le plus important penseur soviètique dans le domaine des sciences humaines et le plus grand théoricien de la littérature au $20^{\text{ème}}$ siècle" ("the most important Soviet thinker in the area of the human sciences and the greatest literary theorist of the twentieth century")

(Todorov), and "as one of the leading thinkers of the 20th century" (Michael Holquist). In both cases, this entirely justified admiration is focused on Bakhtin's contribution to the theory of the novel, not only in the relatively well-known books on Rabelais and Dostoevsky but in more theoretical studies such as the essay entitled "Discourse in the Novel" which dates from 1934-1935. This essay is singled out by both Todorov and Holquist as the major theoretical statement. And, within the theory of the novel, it is the concept of dialogism, rather than related but other Bakhtinian terms such as chronotope, refraction, heteroglossia or the carnivalesque, that receives major attention, as is apparent from the titles of the two books *Le principe dialogique* (1981) and *The Dialogic Imagination* (1981).[2]

The last thing I wish to do here is to dispute or dispel this enthusiasm. There is no merit whatever to the facile and always cheaply available gesture that protects mediocrity by exposing the blindness that is part of any dedication and of the admiration it inspires. The attentive and critical reading of Bakhtin's work has barely begun, at least in the West, and since I ignore the Russian language, it is not an enterprise in which I can responsibly hope to take part. My question therefore does not address the significance of Bakhtin, or Voloshinov-Bakhtin or of Medvedev-Bakhtin, as a theoretician or as a thinker, but the much more narrow question of why the notion of dialogism can be so enthusiastically received by theoreticians of very diverse persuasion and made to appear as a valid way out of many of the quandaries that have plagued us for so long. Or, to put it in the terms of this issue: how does dialogism, as developed in Bakhtin and his group, cope with and indeed seem to overcome the ever-recurring question of the status of the referent in works of fiction?

Dialogism can mean, and indeed has meant, many things to many critics, sometimes without reference to Bakhtin. Its more or less submerged presence is noticeable in the papers presented in this issue, as when Hilary Putnam invites us to see criticism as "a conversation with many voices rather than as a contest with winners and losers." It can, first of all, simply mean double-talk, the necessary obliqueness of any persecuted speech that cannot, at the risk of survival, openly say what it means to say: there is ample evidence, from what is known of Bakhtin's biography, that this meaning is entirely relevant in his case. The readers of oppressed thinkers, in the words of a major theoretician of the discourse of persecution, "are to be led step to step from the popular view . . . to the truth which is merely and purely theoretical, guided by certain obtrusively enigmatic features in the presentation of the popular teaching — obscurity of the plan, contradictions, pseudonyms, inexact repetitions of earlier statements, strange expressions, etc." This quotation from Leo Strauss's *Persecution and the Art of Writing*[3] fits the case of Bakhtin very well. Strauss could have added another salient feature: the circulation of more or less clandestine class or seminar notes by initiated disciples or, even more symptomatic, the rumored (and often confirmed) existence of unpublished manuscripts made available only to an enterprising or privileged researcher and which will decisively seal one mode of interpretation at the expense of all rival modes — at least until one of the rivals will, in his turn, discover the real or imaginary counter-manuscript on which to base his counterclaim. What in the context of our topic interests us primarily in this situation is that it is bound to engender a community tied together by the common task of decrypting the repressed message hidden in the public utterance. As the sole detainers of an esoteric knowledge, this community is bound to be small, self-selective, and likely to consider itself as a chosen elite. To the extent, however, that the process of understanding becomes constitutively linked to the elaboration and the life of a society, fact and fiction are brought together by the mediation of shared communal labor. The possibility of a mediation between sign and referent within the production of the text itself; since it does not mean to say what it actually says, it is a fiction, but a fiction that, in the hands of the right community of readers, will become fact.

For Leo Strauss, the model of persecution applies predominantly to philosophical rather than to literary texts; Bakhtin's stress on the novel adds a potentially libertarian and revolutionary dimension. "Im Sklaven fängt die Prosa an": it is in the slave, says Hegel, that prose begins and he says this in the section of the *Aesthetics* that deals precisely with fables as the ancestors of the novel. Like Strauss's philosopher, Bakhtin's novelist is persecuted per definition and carries within himself the image of his liberation. But this image exists not, as is still the case in Lukács, in the form of a nostalgia for the presumably unified world of the epic; the novelist does not set out to take the place of his master, the epic poet, but to set him free from the restricting coercions of his single-minded, monological vision. Bakhtin's novel definitely belongs to what Northrop Frye calls the low-mimetic modes: it is ideologically prosaic, anti-romance, anti-epical and anti-mythical; its multivoicedness or heteroglossia postulates distinct and antagonistic class structures as well as the celebratory crossing of social barriers. The dialogism of a revolutionary community reconciles fact and fiction in a manner that is not essentially distinct from the persecutory model, except for the introduction of a temporal dimension: the freedom that is being celebrated is not utopian, yet it is not actualized in the immediacy of the textual invention. It is projected in a metatextual future as the prolepsis of a no longer fictional freedom. The scheme is bound to exercise a powerful attraction on a type of literary criticism that stems from a rebellion against the constraints of transcendental and monological systems such as institutional religions. An author and a concept — dialogism — that can be made to accommodate the textual model of Leo Strauss (persecution) as well as of some disciples of Gilles Deleuze (celebration) shows, to say the least, remarkable scope.

In Bakhtin's writings, the notion of dialogism is also systematically developed, not only, as in "Discourse in the Novel" or in the Rabelais book, in dialectical exchange with the persecutory power of monistic discourses, but in a prolonged and complex discussion of formalism. As is well known, the topic figures prominently in the pseudonymous books *Marxism and the Philosophy of Language* (Vološinov) and *The Formal Method in Literary Scholarship* (Medvedev). Very summarily put, it is possible to think of dialogism as a still formal method by which to conquer or to sublate formalism itself. Dialogism is here still a descriptive and metalinguistic term that says something about language rather than about the world. Bakhtin is consistent in his assertion that the dialogical relationship is intra-linguistic, between what he calls two heterogeneous "voices," as in a musical score. It is, in his terms, the image of a *language* (p. 354) — rather than the *image* of a language — and not of a society or of an interpersonal relationship. Therefore, as becomes evident in examples taken from Dickens and Turgenev, it is possible to analyze descriptively dialogical structures in actual texts, in a manner that is by no means unusual to "formalist" practitioners of an American style of close reading. On the other hand, dialogism also functions, throughout the work and especially in the Dostoevsky book, as a principle of radical otherness or, to use again Bakhtin's own terminology, as a principle of *exotopy*: far from aspiring to the telos of a synthesis or a resolution, as could be said to be the case in dialectical systems, the function of dialogism is to sustain and think through the radical exteriority or heterogeneity of one voice with regard to any other, including that of the novelist himself. She or he is not, in this regard, in any privileged situation with respect to his characters. The self-reflexive, autotelic or, if you wish, narcissistic structure of form, as a definitional description enclosed within specific borderlines, is hereby replaced by an *assertion* of the otherness of the other, preliminary to even the possibility of a *recognition* of his otherness. Rather than having to do with class structures, as in the societal models of "Discourse in the Novel," exotopy has to do with relationships between distinct cultural and ideological units. It would apply to conflicts between nations or religions rather than between classes. In this perspective, dialogism is no longer a formal and descriptive principle, nor does it pertain particularly to language: heteroglossia (multi-variedness between discourses) is a special case of exotopy (otherness as such) and the formal study of literary texts becomes important because it leads from intralinguistic to intracultural relationships. At that point, the binary opposition between fiction and fact is no longer relevant: in any differential system, it is the assertion of the space *between* the entities that matters. Binaries, to the extent that they allow and invite synthesis, are therefore the most misleading of differential structures. Novelists like Dostoevsky or, one might surmise, Balzac reveal their exotopy when they simply ignore such strongly suggestive oppositions as those between author and character: Dostoevsky's or Balzac's characters are not voices of authorial identity or identification (not: *Madame Bovary, c'est moi*) but voices of radical alterity, not because they are fictions and the author isn't, but because their otherness *is* their reality. The reality principle coincides with the principle of otherness. Bakhtin at times conveys the impression that one can accede from dialogism as a metalinguistic (i.e., formal) structure to dialogism as a recognition of exotopy. The itinerary beyond form by ways of formal analysis is particularly attractive to someone skilled in the formal analysis of structural semiotics or structural stylistics but grown impatient with the inability to break out of the formal shell and to address, at long last, questions that appear no longer to be merely linguistic. Todorov is, of course, himself a case in point.

It is also by ways of exotopy that, finally, a larger philosophical claim can be made for Bakhtin as not just a technician of literary discourse but as a thinker or metaphysician whose name can be considered next to those of Husserl, Heidegger or, as Todorov aptly suggests, Levinas. The radical experience of voiced otherness as a way to a regained proximity can indeed be found as a dominant theme in Levinas and to have at least a submerged existence in Heidegger. One can think of the lines in Hölderlin, *"Seit ein Gespräch wir sind / Und hören können voneinander"* as a common ground. Whether the passage from otherness to the recognition of the other, the passage, in other words, from dialogism to dialogue, can be said to take place in Bakhtin as more than a desire, remains a question for Bakhtin interpretation to consider in the proper critical spirit. This renders premature any more specific consideration of how this recognition is to occur as a religious transcendentalism which would allow one to read "God" wherever Bakhtin says "society," as a Heideggerian disclosure of ontological truth in the otherness of language or as a secular but messianic ideologism that would bear a superficial, and perhaps misleading, resemblance to the position attributed to Walter Benjamin. To adjudicate hastily between the various options would be unthinkable; what can be observed is that, in each case, dialogism appears as a provisional stage under way toward a more absolute claim, a claim that is not necessarily monological but that points, at any rate, well beyond the limited confines of literary theory. Whether such an extension of Bakhtin's range is sound and legitimate also remains to be established. But that it is a possibility is made clear by the tone, even more than by the substance, of what is being written about him in Western Europe and in the United States.

One sees that it would be possible to line up an impressive list of contemporary theorists of very diverse persuasion, all of which would have a legitimate claim on Bakhtin's dialogism as congenial or even essential to their enterprise: the list could include analytical philosophers, formalist semioticians grown weary with their science, narratologists, technicians of reader reception, religious phenomenologists, Heideggerian critical ontologists, defenders of permanent revolution, disciples of Leo Strauss — and one could easily play the game of extending still further this list of unlikely bedfellows. If one then would be curious to know what they have in common, at least negatively, one should perhaps ask who, if anyone, would have reason to find it difficult or even impossible to enlist Bakhtin's version of dialogism among his methodological tools or skills. Such as, for example, a literary theoretician or critic concerned with tropological displacements of logic, with a rhetoric of cognition as well as of persuasion. Bakhtin has very astute things to say about tropes but, if one is willing to suspend for a moment the potential dialogical otherness of these statements, he seems, on the whole, to consider that the discourse of tropes is not dialogical, does not account for dialogism and remains, by and large, on the near side of the theories of narrative that dialogism allows one to elaborate. Bakhtin frequently asserts the separation of trope from dialogism, for instance in the passage on the distinction between discourse in poetry and in prose, as stated in terms of refraction, in "Discourse" or in the later, even more dogmatically explicit passage in the same text, on the distinction between the tropological polysemy of poetry and the dialogism of prose. Here Bakhtin unambiguously asserts that "no matter how one understands the interrelationship of meanings in a poetic symbol (a trope), this interrelationship is never of the dialogic sort; it is impossible under any conditions or at any time to imagine a trope (say, a metaphor) being unfolded into the two exchanges of a dialogue, that is, two meanings parceled out between two separate voices" (pp. 327-28). These passages are among the richest in the canon of Bakhtin's works, but this implies that they are also among the most contradictory and, for that reason, monologically aberrant. More than any other, they reveal the metaphysical *impensé* of Bakhtin's thought, the dogmatic foundations that make the dialogical ideology so attractive and so diverse. This is not the time and the place for a detailed analysis of the passages in question. But lest you suspect me of being evasive, let me state the direction that such a reading would take — while adding, as a matter of course, that at the moment when I appropriate these passages as the ground of my own admiration for the revealingly aberrant character of Bakhtin's writings, I have included myself in the odd list of Bakhtin admirers from which I first pretended to be excluded; this, however, in no way disposes of the negative thrust of the proposed argument. One would have to point out (1) that, for Bakhtin, the trope is an intentional structure directed toward an object and, as such, a pure *episteme* and not a fact of language; this in fact excludes tropes from literary discourse, poetic as well as prosaic, and locates them, perhaps surprisingly, in the field of epistemology; (2) that the opposition between trope as object-directed and dialogism as social-oriented discourse sets up a binary opposition between object and society that is itself tropological in the worst possible sense, namely as a reification; (3) and more revealing for us, that as the analysis of dialogical refraction develops, Bakhtin has to reintroduce the categorical foundations of a precritical phenomenalism in which there is no room for exotopy, for otherness, in any shape or degree. When it is said, for example, that "the heteroglot voices . . . create the background necessary for [the author's] own voice" (p. 278), we recognize the foreground-background model derived from Husserl's theories of perception and here uncritically assimilating the structure of language to the structure of a secure perception: from that moment on, the figure of refraction and of the light ray becomes coercive as the only possible trope for trope, and we are within a reflective system of *mise en abyme* that is anything but dialogical. It is therefore not at all surprising that, still in the same passage, Bakhtin modulates irrevocably from dialogism to a conception of dialogue as question and answer of which it can then be said that "the speaker breaks through the alien conceptual horizon of the listener, constructs his own utterance on alien territory, against his, the listener's, apperceptive background" (p. 282). Again, there is no trace of dialogism left in such a gesture of dialectical imperialism that is an inevitable part of any hermeneutic system of question and answer. The ideologies of otherness and of hermeneutic understanding are not compatible, and therefore their relationship is not a dialogical but simply a contradictory one. It is not a foregone conclusion whether Bakhtin's discourse is itself dialogical or simply contradictory.

Let me turn, in conclusion, to a text which can, I think, be said to be dialogical, which also happens to be a dialogue and a dialogue about the novel at that. Rousseau's prefatory post-face to *La Nouvelle Héloise*, sometimes entitled *Dialogue on the Novel*, combines two modes of dialogue. First a hermeneutic mode in which author and reader are engaged in a sequence of questions and answers, a set of whos and whats for the purpose of determining whether the contents of the novel are fact or fiction: who is Julie? did she exist? etc. The outcome of this hermeneutic quest, like the outcome of the session at the MLA that resulted in this issue, is utterly inconclusive: the hermeneutics of reference are undecidable. But, in case you worry about the legitimacy of our present performance, the decision of undecidability is itself entirely rational and legitimate: although another session on fact and fiction within the novel in next year's MLA is not going to get any further than we got today, such a continuation is entirely legitimate and, in fact, inevitable. The formal expression of this certainty is manifest in the symmetry of the question and answer patterns which would allow one, within the orbit of such a question, to substitute author for reader without any loss of consistency: the unreadability of the referent is just as challenging, and for the same reasons, for the one as for the other, and their complicity in the hermeneutic quest is manifest.

On the other hand, the text also stages something very different: a battle of wits between author and reader in which they try to outdo each other, parrying, feinting, and setting traps in a sequence of attacks and defenses somewhat like a fencing match, or like the seduction which is being carried on in the exchange of letters that make up the first part of Rousseau's novel. In this exchange, the question is no longer a question of who or what: it would be naive to ask who wins the match since in this model, Rousseau, as author, controls the moves of each of the antagonists. And it would be equally naive to ask over what one is fighting: one fights over whether or not there is a question, which means that one is at least twice removed from any possibility of an answer as to what, in this fight, is at stake. All the interest focuses on *how* one fights (or seduces), on the how, the *poetics* of writing and of reading rather than the hermeneutics. The author wants to know what all authors always want to know: did you read my book? did you read it to the end? do you think people will want to buy it? will it sell in Paris? all of which amounts to wondering if he put it together right — questions all belonging to the realm of empirical poetics (how to write a book that will achieve fame) rather than hermeneutics (what is the truth of the text). This puts him at an obvious disadvantage in the ensuing battle in which the urbane reader can constantly play on the vulnerability of his position and make him look foolish: the smart reader always outwits an author who depends on him from the moment he has opened a dialogue that is never entirely gratuitous, that is always a battle for mastery. Yet, at the end of Rousseau's text, the character designated by *R* and who is the author, refuses the substitution offered to him:

N. . . . I advise you, however, to switch parts. Pretend that I am the one who urges you on to publish this collection of letters and that you are the one who resists. You give yourself the objections and I'll rebut them. It will sound more humble and make a better impression.

R. Will it also be in conformity with what you find to be praiseworthy in my character?

N. No, I was setting you a trap. Leave things as they are.[4]

One of the ways in which this tricky passage has to be read is as the refusal, in terms of poetics, to grant the substitutive symmetry implied in a hermeneutics. Rousseau does not have the least intention to relinquish to his reader the benefit in fame or money of the 70,000 copies which, at the time of writing the so-called preface, he knew his novel had already sold, in Paris as well as in the provinces. *Rira bien qui rira le dernier*. This success of his poetics is in no way compatible, however, with the rules of his hermeneutics. The relationship between poetics and hermeneutics, like that between *R* the author and *N* the reader, is dialogical to the precise extent that the one cannot be substituted for the other, despite the fact that the non-dialogical discourse of question and answer fully justifies the substitution. What one has to admire Bakhtin for (that is, want to be in his place in having written what he wrote), as all his present readers, including myself, do, is his hope that by starting out, as he does, in a poetics of novelistic discourse one may gain access to the power of a hermeneutics. The apparent question of the relationship between fact and fiction in the novel hides the more fundamental question of the compatibility between the descriptive discourse of poetics and the normative discourse of hermeneutics. Such compatibility can only be achieved at the expense of dialogism. To imitate or to apply Bakhtin, to read him by engaging him in a dialogue, betrays what is most valid in his work.

Notes

1. This essay originally appeared in an issue of *Poetics Today* 4:1 (1983) entitled "Reference and Fictionality," containing contributions to a 1981 MLA Forum, "Fiction and Its Referents: A Reappraisal."

2. Tzvetan Todorov, *Mikhail Bakhtin: The Dialogical Principle*, Wlad Godsich, trans. (Minneapolis: University of Minnesota Press, 1984); Michael Holquist, ed., *The Dialogic Imagination: Four Essays by Mikhail Bakhtin*, Caryl Emerson and Michael Holquist, trans. (Austin: University of Texas Press, 1981). Citations from the latter will be identified by page number within the text.

3. Leo Strauss, *Persecution and the Art of Writing* (Westport: "Greenwood" Press, 1973 [1952]), p. 36.

4. J. J. Rousseau, *Oeuvres complètes*, B. Gagnebin and M. Raymond, eds. (Paris: Gallimard, Bibliothèque de la Pléiade, 1978), vol. 2, p. 30.

An Interview with Paul de Man
Stefano Rosso

Rosso: You have been educated in Europe and have taught both in Europe and the U.S.: what kind of implications for your understanding of "pedagogy" did you derive from this experience?

de Man: I have been teaching in the United States for the last thirty years and it's an experience which I take so much for granted that I don't reflect on it very much anymore. I became aware of it because for a time I taught alternatively at the University of Zurich, at Cornell, and at Hopkins. I had then the possibility to compare the situation of teaching in Europe and of teaching here: in Europe one is of course much closer to ideological and political questions, while, on the contrary, in the States, one is much closer to professional questions. So the ethics of the profession are very different. I found it difficult in Europe to be teaching material that was so separated from the actual professional use that students, who were mostly destined to teach in secondary school, would make

This interview was granted by de Man on March 4, 1983 after the last of the "Messenger Lectures" he gave at Cornell University. The interview was commissioned by the RAI (the Italian National Broadcasting System) — it was broadcast in Italy on June 1, 1983 — and de Man had agreed to try to be as "perspicuous" as possible, since he had to be understood by listeners and not by professional readers. I have decided to leave the text in its original form in order not to lose its oral "awkwardness." An Italian translation of part of this text appeared in *Alfabeta* 58 (March 1984), p. 12. I wish to thank Raffaello Siniscalco of the RAI Corporation for permission to print this text, and Christopher Fynsk and David Randall for their advice in preparing the interview. A special thanks to Giuseppe Mazzotta, who convinced de Man to grant me the interview, and to Philip Lewis, who placed his office at our disposal — Stefano Rosso.

of it. So there was a real discrepancy between what one talked about and what the use value of this could be for the students. So it had a very special feeling of alienation to me, very differently from here, where since one teaches future colleagues, one has a very direct professional relationship to them — which, however, has its own ideologies and its own politics, which are more the politics of the profession, the relationship of the academic profession to the American political world and society. I ended up finding the function of teaching in the United States — the function of an academic as distinct from the academic function — much more satisfactory than in Europe, precisely because of the contract one has with the people one teaches. Here you can actually carry out your contractual relation to them, whereas in Europe you can't. In Europe there is a bizarre separation on two completely different levels. It's concretely visible in the fact that you stand up there, on that chair, with an abyss between you and the students, while here you sit at a table. I found bad faith involved in that ideological situation in Europe, worse than here. It is slightly more honest here, though certainly the political problem then gets transposed to the relationship between the "academic" and society at large. I found it easier to cope with that than with what one faces in Europe . . .

Rosso: How can you explain the success of Derrida's work and more generally of deconstruction in the American academic world?

de Man: I think part of the success of Derrida (well, the relative success, which has to be qualified) is that, unlike most of the other French critics, he works very close to texts, he *reads* very attentively, and both American teachers and students of literature are better prepared for that sort of thing than Europeans because of the discipline of the New Criticism and of close reading. There is something in Derrida which is more familiar, but, on the other hand, a great deal more exciting than certain techniques which are used, so that Derrida's close working with specific texts is something that makes him certainly more accessible to the American audience, both in a positive sense — in the sense that people can continue from what he does — and in a negative sense — to the extent that, by his concentration on texts and on a canon of texts which is relatively traditional, he can and has indeed been attacked for being too close to textual works, and addressing more problems of textual interpretation than problems of a political or of a more general nature. Frequently, the difference between Foucault and Derrida and the attempts to bring the two together focus precisely on this question of close reading of texts, so that his success is ambivalent and is also a cause for criticism. It is also a little bit in those terms that the relationship between Derrida and what is called American "Derridism or Derridianism" is often discussed. It is often said — and this is true to some extent — that whatever is audacious, whatever is really subversive and incisive in Derrida's text and in his work is being taken out by academizing him, by making him just one other method by means of which literature can be taught. And there is an element in Derrida which lends itself to that, because we can find in Derrida exemplary ways of reading, an awareness, for example, of rhetorical complexities in a text which are applicable to the didactics, to the pedagogy of literary teaching, and as such there is an impact of Derrida which is, in a sense, purely pedagogical. As far as I'm concerned, I'm often mentioned as the one who is much responsible for that, since my work is, in a sense, more pedagogical than philosophical: it has always started from the pedagogical or the didactic assignment of reading specific texts rather than, as is the case in Derrida, from the pressure of general philosophical issues. I can see some merit to that statement, except for the fact that I don't think it is possible, in Derrida, to separate the classical didactic pedagogical element, which is undeniably there, from the subversive aspect of his work. To the extent that Derrida has this classical discipline in him, his subversion is particularly effective, much more so, I think, in this case, than in the case of somebody like Foucault, who directly addresses political issues, but without an awareness of the textual complexities that lead up to it, although Foucault has an almost intuitive awareness of them . . . . So, personally, I don't have a bad conscience when I'm being told that, to the extent that it is didactic, my work is academic or even, as it is used as a supreme insult, it is just more New Criticism. I can live with that very easily, because I think that only what is, in a sense, classically didactic, can be really and effectively subversive. And I think the same applies there to Derrida. Which doesn't mean that there are not essential differences: Derrida feels compelled to say more about the institution of the university, but that is more understandable within the European context, where the university has such a predominating cultural function, whereas in the United States it has no cultural function at all, here it is not inscribed in the genuine cultural tensions of the nation . . . .

Rosso: Can you say something more about the differences between your work and Derrida's?

de Man: I'm not really the right person to ask where the difference is, because, as I feel in many respects close to Derrida, I don't determine whether my work resembles or is different from that of Derrida. My initial engagement with Derrida — which I think is typical and important for all that relationship (to the extent that I can think or want to think about it at all) which followed closely upon my first encounter with him in Baltimore at the colloquium on ''The Languages of Criticism and the Sciences of Man'' — had not to do with Derrida or with me, but with Rousseau. It happened that we were both working on Rousseau and basically on the same text, by sheer coincidence. It was in relation to Rousseau that I was anxious to define, to try to work out some — not discrepancies — but some change of emphasis between what Derrida does and what I'm doing. And there may be something in that difference between us that remained there, to the extent that in a very genuine sense — not as denegation or as false modesty (though whenever one says "not out of denegation" one is awaking the suspicion to be even more denying than before . . . so you can't get out of that bind . . .) — my starting point, as I think I already told you, is not philosophical but basically philological and for that reason didactical, text-oriented. Therefore I have a tendency to put upon texts an inherent authority, which is stronger, I think, than Derrida is willing to put on them. I assume, as a working hypothesis (as a working hypothesis, because I know better than that), that the text *knows* in an absolute way what it's doing. I know this is not the case, but it is a necessary working hypothesis that Rousseau knows at any time what he is doing and as such there is no need to deconstruct Rousseau. In a complicated way, I would hold to that statement that "the text deconstructs itself, is self-deconstructive" rather than being deconstructed by a philosophical intervention from the outside of the text. The difference is that Derrida's text is so brilliant, so incisive, so strong that whatever happens in Derrida, it happens between him and his own text. He doesn't need Rousseau, he doesn't need anybody else; I do need them very badly because I never had an idea of my own, it was always through a text, through the critical examination of a text . . . I am a philologist and not a philosopher: I guess there is a difference there . . . . I think that, on the other hand, it is of some interest to see how the two different approaches can occasionally coincide, at the point that Gasché in the two articles he has written on this topic (and which are together with an article by Godzich certainly the best things that have been written on it) says that Derrida and myself are the closest when I do not use his terminology, and the most remote when I use terms such as *deconstruction*: I agree with that entirely. But, again, I am not the one to decide on this particular matter and I don't claim to be on that level. . . .

Rosso: Do you agree with Lentricchia when, in his *After the New Criticism*, he speaks about a strong influence of Sartre on your work? And how was your first encounter with the work of Heidegger?

de Man: In factual terms, just to get the facts straight, like all people of my generation, that is people who were twenty years old when the war began, Sartre was very important. What interested me most in Sartre were literary-critical texts that appeared in *Situations 1* and specifically the text on Ponge, that on Jules Renard, within which Sartre does very close textual work and talks about texts in a way which then was quite new. (There was also an earlier article by Sartre which had to do with point of view . . . an attack on Flaubert). I remember those articles very well and I've been much impressed by them. They are, however, articles which are very comparable, let's say, to the New Criticism. They are articles which are very formalistic and which are close-reading in a very technical way, which Sartre, later on, did not pursue. I was at the same time, however, much more influenced by all people who generally came from the tradition of Surrealism, specifically Bataille, Blanchot, even critics like Bachelard who were working in a very different vein than Sartre. And in the slight opposition which became visible, for example, in the debate that developed between Sartre and Blanchot — in Sartre's piece on *Qu'est-ce que la littérature* which was very much read and discussed, to which Blanchot then wrote a kind of answer which was called *La littérature et le droit à la mort* — I felt myself, if you can put it in those simple terms, more on the side of Blanchot than of Sartre. So, certainly, I was not simply influenced by Sartre, but one would have to put many names next to Sartre and this would be again typical of my generation: there would be other names and it would only be some aspects of Sartre.

In the specific case of Heidegger, I began to have some awareness of his work during the war and soon afterward, first through a monograph by a Belgian philosopher called De Waelhens, who during the war published a book on Heidegger. Then, whatever influence I got from that, it did not come through Sartre. I always felt that the use made of Heidegger, and also to a lesser extent of Husserl, in Sartre missed the mark, and on the occasion of the publication of texts like Heidegger's *Letter on Humanism*, which was much discussed at that time, and which was, in a sense, polemical to Sartre, there too felt closer to whatever Heidegger was saying. So it seems to me slightly far-fetched to speak of a specific influence of Sartre. . . . But Sartre — even Derrida told me that about himself — for many of us was the first encounter with some kind of philosophical language which was not just academic. So it was the fact that Sartre wrote essays like *L'imaginaire, L'être et le néant*, which were technical philosophical books, while at the same time being a literary critic, at the same time being somebody who expressed strong opinions on political matters — that somewhat mythological bicephalic dissent of the philosopher — had a very strong attraction; I don't think anybody of my generation ever got over that. We all somehow would like to be like that: it takes about a whole life to get over this notion, and I suppose the attraction of people like Bataille, whose relationship to the political (because they were very political) was more complex, more mediated, than in the case of Sartre, was a way to resist the obvious attraction of Sartre's flamboyant presence on the scene — Sartre and Camus, to a lesser extent, but especially Sartre to the extent that he was both a philosopher and an actively engaged political man. But one lost some of the confidence in that figure fairly soon, I think, in terms of certain obvious possible weaknesses in Sartre's work, both on the literary and on the philosophical side.

Rosso: One can notice, in the bibliography of your works, a tendency to neglect contemporary literature: for example, you don't look interested at all in a debate somehow fashionable, the debate about the notion of "postmodernism." . . .

de Man: The difficulty for me is that the "postmodern approach" seems a somewhat naively historical approach. The notion of modernity is already very dubious; the notion of postmodernity becomes a parody of the notion of modernity. It is like the *Nouvelle Revue Française*, the *Nouvelle Nouvelle Revue Française*, the New Criticism, the New New Criticism, etc. It is a bottomless pit that does attempt to define the literary moment in terms of its increased modernity (this happens in the work of Hassan, too). It strikes me as a very unmodern, a very old-fashioned, conservative concept of history, where history is seen as a succession, so that the historical model that is being used at that moment is very dubious and, in a sense, naive, very simple. This applies more to the theoreticians of literature who feel the need to align their work with contemporary work in fiction, who have the slight intimidation which critics sometimes feel in relation to so-called creative authors and who would like to be in harmony with them. I am sure some of that exists in Europe. For me a model like that of Blanchot remains very revealing because he was a critic who was also a writer, and who was not concerned at all as a critic to justify himself as a writer, or as a writer to concern himself as a critic. Interestingly, in the same man you don't have the same subject, you don't have any intention to coordinate whatever is so-called creative without for that matter being in relation to the other, and he could bring them together in some later texts without any difficulty. There was no feeling of inferiority of the critic toward the writer. And that model, which is frequent in France, and which is the model that you have in Mallarmé, is closer to me than the notion of the critic who wants a little bit "to cash in," so to speak, on the certain innovative freedom that a writer can have. I don't know if now the innovation of writers in the States or in France or elsewhere is closer or similar to whatever is being done by literary theorists. And in a fairly categorical way the question does not interest me. If it turns out to be similar, okay, but it certainly would not be — certainly not, in my case and not, I think, in the case of any literary theoretician worth his salt — by trying to pattern himself or by trying to catch what's going on for this moment in the so-called creative fiction as opposed to criticism. . . . I feel perfectly at ease writing on eighteenth- or seventeenth-century authors and don't feel at all compelled to write on contemporaries. On the other hand, there are all kinds of contemporaries, some I feel very close to and some I feel millions of miles removed from . . . .

Rosso: Well, just to make an example, many years ago you wrote an article on Borges . . .

de Man: Well, it was suggested to me . . . . Certainly I would be at any time ready to write on Borges, certainly on the fiction of Blanchot, but if you ask me on what contemporary French authors . . . I could possibly think of myself writing on Calvino, though I might be wrong . . . .

Rosso: Perhaps, now, you could tell us something about the book you are writing and about the "mysterious" chapters on Kierkegaard and Marx you mentioned in the lectures, and the frequent recurrence of the terms "ideology" and "politics" we have noticed recently . . . .

de Man: I don't think I ever was away from these problems, they were always uppermost in my mind. I have always maintained that one could approach the problems of ideology and by extension the problems of politics only on the basis of critical-linguistic analysis, which had to be done in its own terms, in the medium of language, and I felt I could approach those problems only after having achieved a certain control over those questions. It seems pretentious to say so, but it is not the case. I have the feeling I have achieved some control over technical problems of language, specifically problems of rhetoric, of the relation between tropes and performatives, of saturation of tropology as a field that in certain forms of language goes beyond that field. . . . I feel now some control of a vocabulary and of a conceptual apparatus that can handle that. It was in working on Rousseau that I felt I was able to progress from purely linguistic analysis to questions which are really already of a political and ideological nature. So that now I feel to do it a little more openly, though in a very different way than what generally passes as "critique of ideology." It is taking me back to Adorno and to attempts that have been made in that direction in Germany, to certain aspects of Heidegger, and I just feel that one has to face therefore the difficulty of certain explicitly political texts. It is also taking me back constantly to problems having to do with theology and with religious discourse, and that's why the juxtaposition of Marx and Kierkegaard as the two main readers of Hegel appears to me as the crux, as the problem one has, in a way, to solve. I have not solved it and the fact that I keep announcing that I am going to do something about it is only to force myself to do so, because if I keep saying I'm going to do this and I don't do it, I end up looking very foolish. So I have to force myself a little to do this, both in the case of Kierkegaard and in the case of Marx. It's taking me first of all in a preparatory move, by forcing me to go back to Hegel and Kant, and I just hope that I won't remain stuck in that. So I felt ready to say something about the problem of ideology, not out of a polemical urge. What has been said about it, what now is around in the books of Jameson or of other people, is not what spurred me to do this. As I said, it has always been a major concern and I now feel this problem of language somewhat more under control. What will come out of it, I just do not know because I do not work that way. What will come out, will come from the texts of Marx and Kierkegaard as I think they will have to be read. And they have to be read from the perspective of critical-linguistic analysis to which those texts have not been submitted. There has been very little on Kierkegaard along those lines and there has been even less on Marx, except, of course, for elements in Althusser that, I think, go in that direction. But I look foward to seeing what I will produce and know as little about it as anybody else.

Bibliography of Texts by Paul de Man
Tom Keenan

●

"I would never have by myself undertaken the task of establishing such a collection [. . .]. Such massive evidence of the failure to make the various individual readings coalesce is a somewhat melancholy spectacle. The fragmentary aspect of the whole is made more obvious still by the hypotactic manner that prevails in each of the essays taken in isolation, by the continued attempt, however ironized, to present a closed and linear argument. This apparent coherence *within* each essay is not matched by a corresponding coherence *between* them. Laid out diachronically in a roughly chronological sequence, they do not evolve in a manner that easily allows for dialectical progression or, ultimately, for historical totalization. Rather, it seems that they always start again from scratch and that their conclusions fail to add up to anything." Paul de Man, "Preface," *The Rhetoric of Romanticism*, viii.

Books

Blindness and Insight: Essays in the Rhetoric of Contemporary Criticism. New York: Oxford University Press, 1971 [noted here as BI]. Second edition, with five additional essays, edited by Wlad Godzich, Minneapolis: University of Minnesota Press, 1983 [noted here as BI2]. First edition, with additional essays, translated into Serbo-Croatian by Gordana B. Todorović and Branko Jelić as *Problemi Moderne Kritike*, Beograd: Nolit, 1975; translated into Italian, with "The Rhetoric of Temporality," by Eduardo Saccone and Giancarlo Mazzacurati, as *Cecità e visione: Linguaggio letterario e critica contemporanea*, Napoli: Liguori, 1975.

Allegories of Reading: Figural Language in Rousseau, Nietzsche, Rilke, and Proust. New Haven: Yale University Press, 1979 [noted here as AR]. French and German translations forthcoming.

The Rhetoric of Romanticism. New York: Columbia University Press, 1984 [noted here as RR].

The Resistance to Theory. Edited and with an introduction by Wlad Godzich. Minneapolis: University of Minnesota Press, 1986 [noted here as RT].

122

Articles, Translations, etc.

1. "Le roman anglais contemporain," *Les Cahiers du Libre Examen* 4:4, January 1940, 16-19.
2. "Littérature française," *Les Cahiers du Libre Examen* 4:5, February 1940, 34-35.
3. Translation of Paul Alverdes, *Le double visage* [Das Zweigesicht]. Brussels-Paris: Editions de la Toison d'Or, 1942.
4. Translation of Filip de Pillecyn [Pillecijn], *Le soldat Johan*. Brussels-Paris: Editions de la Toison d'Or, 1942.
5. *Les dessins de Paul Valéry*, "texte de P. de Man." Paris: Les Editions Universelles, 1948. [Text: ix-xxxv, drawings: xli-cxi. Authorship not confirmed.]
6. "Jacques Villon," *Konstrevy* 28:3, 1952, 133-38. ["By P. de Man," authorship not confirmed. In Swedish.]
7. "Montaigne et la transcendance," *Critique* 79, December 1953, 1011-22.
8. "The Inward Generation," *i.e., The Cambridge Review* 1:2, Winter 1955, 41-47.
9. "Le néant poétique (commentaire d'un sonnet hermétique de Mallarmé)," *Monde Nouveau* 88, April 1955, 63-75.
10. "Tentation de la permanence," *Monde Nouveau* 93, October 1955, 49-61. Translated by Don Latimer as "The Temptation of Permanence," *Southern Humanities Review* 17:3, Summer 1983, 209-21.
11. "Les exégèses de Hölderlin par Martin Heidegger," *Critique* 100-01, September-October 1955, 800-19. Translated by Wlad Godzich as "Heidegger's Exegeses of Hölderlin," Chapter 12 in BI2, 246-66.
12. "Keats and Hölderlin," *Comparative Literature* 8:1, Winter 1956, 28-45.
13. "Impasse de la critique formaliste," *Critique* 109, June 1956, 438-500. Translated by Wlad Godzich as "The Dead-End of Formalist Criticism," Chapter 11 in BI2, 229-45.
14. "Situation de roman," *Monde Nouveau* 101, June 1956, 57-60.
15. "Le devenir, la poésie," *Monde Nouveau* 105, November 1956, 110-24.
16. "La critique thématique devant le theme de Faust," *Critique* 120, May 1957, 387-404.
17. Translation of Martin Heidegger, "Hölderlin and the Essence of Poetry [Hölderlin und das Wesen der Dichtung]," *Quarterly Review of Literature* 10:1-2, 1959, 79-94. Reprinted in T. and R. Weiss, ed., *QRL: Special Issues Retrospective* 20:1-2, 1976, 456-71.
18. *Mallarmé, Yeats and the Post-Romantic Predicament*, Ph.D. dissertation, Comparative Literature, Harvard University, May 1960, v + 316 page typescript. One portion excerpted by de Man as "Image and Emblem in Yeats," Chapter 8 in RR, 145-238.
19. "Structure intentionelle de l'image romantique," *Revue internationale de philosophie* 51, 1960, 68-84. Translated by de Man, slightly revised, as "Intentional Structure of the Romantic Image." In Harold Bloom, ed., *Romanticism and Consciousness*. New York: Norton, 1970, 65-77. Reprinted in M. H. Abrams, ed., *Wordsworth: A Collection of Critical Essays*. Englewood Cliffs, NJ: Prentice-Hall, 1972, 133-44. Reprinted as Chapter 1 in RR, 1-17.
20. "A New Vitalism" [review of Harold Bloom, *The Visionary Company*], *The Massachusetts Review* 3:3, Spring 1962, 618-23.
21. "Symbolic Landscape in Wordsworth and Yeats." In Richard Poirier and Reuben Brower, ed., *In Defense of Reading*. New York: Dutton, 1962, 22-37. Reprinted as Chapter 7 in RR, 125-43.
22. "Giraudoux" [review of Jean Giraudoux, *Three Plays*], *The New York Review of Books* 1:7, 28 November 1963, 20-21.
23. "Heidegger Reconsidered" [review of William Barrett, *What is Existentialism?*], *The New York Review of Books* 2:4, 2 April 1964, 14-16.
24. "Spacecritics" [review of J. Hillis Miller, *The Disappearance of God* and Joseph Frank, *The Widening Gyre*], *Partisan Review* 31:4, Fall 1964, 640-50.
25. "Sartre's Confessions" [review of Jean-Paul Sartre, *The Words*], *The New York Review of*

Books 3:7 [sic; actual issue is 3:6], 5 November 1964, 10-13.

26. "A Modern Master" [review of Jorge Luis Borges, *Labyrinths* and *Dreamtigers*], *The New York Review of Books* 3:7, 19 November 1964, 8-10.

27. "Whatever Happened to André Gide" [review of André Gide, *Marshlands* and *Prometheus Misbound* and Wallace Fowlie, *André Gide: His Life and Art*], *The New York Review of Books* 4:7, 6 May 1965, 15-17.

28. "Nihilism" [reply to letter to the editor from Michael P. Scott], *The New York Review of Books* 4:9, 3 June 1965, 26-27. 27.

29. "What is Modern?" [review of Richard Ellmann and Charles Feidelson, eds., *The Modern Tradition*], *The New York Review of Books* 5:2, 26 August 1965, 10-13.

30. "The Mask of Albert Camus" [review of Albert Camus, *Notebooks, 1942-1951*], *The New York Review of Books* 5:10, 23 December 1965, 10-13.

31. "L'image de Rousseau dans la poésie de Hölderlin," *Deutsche Beiträge zur Geistigen Überlieferung* 5, 1965, 157-83. Translated by Renate Böschenstein-Schäfer as "Hölderlins Rousseaubild," *Hölderlin-Jahrbuch* 15, 1967-68, 180-208. Translated by Andrzej Warminski as "The Image of Rousseau in the Poetry of Hölderlin," Chapter 2 in RR, 19-45.

32. Entry under "Modern Poetics: French and German." In Alex Preminger, ed., *Princeton Encyclopedia of Poetry and Poetics*. Princeton: Princeton University Press, 1965, 518-23.

33. "Introduction," to Paul de Man, ed. and trans., Gustave Flaubert, *Madame Bovary*, New York; Norton, 1965, vii-xiii.

34. "Wordsworth und Hölderlin," *Schweizer Monatshefte* 45:12, March 1966, 1141-55. Translated by Timothy Bahti as "Wordsworth and Hölderlin," Chapter 3 in RR, 47-65.

35. "The Literature of Nihilism" [review of Erich Heller, *The Artist's Journey into the Interior and Other Essays* and Ronald Gray, *The German Tradition in Literature, 1871-1945*], *The New York Review of Books* 6:11, 23 June 1966, 16-20.

36. "La circularité de l'interprétation dans l'oeuvre de Maurice Blanchot," *Critique* 229, June 1966, 547-49. Translated by de Man, revised, as "Impersonality in the Criticism of Maurice Blanchot." In John K. Simon, ed., *Modern French Criticism: From Proust to Valéry to Structuralism*. Chicago: University of Chicago Press, 1972, 255-76.

37. "New Criticism et nouvelle critique," *Preuves* 188, October 1966, 29-37. Translated by de Man, revised, as "Form and Intent in the American New Criticism," Chapter 2 in BI, 20-35.

38. "Georg Lukács's *Theory of the Novel*," *MLN* 81:5, December 1966, 527-34. Reprinted as Chapter 4 in BI, 51-59. Reprinted in Richard Macksey, ed., *Velocities of Change: Critical Essays from MLN*. Baltimore: Johns Hopkins University Press, 1974, 207-14.

39. "Madame de Staël and Jean-Jacques Rousseau," *Preuves* 190, December 1966, 35-40.

40. "Introduction," to Paul de Man, ed., John Keats, *Selected Poetry*. New York: Signet (New American Library), 1966, ix-xxxvi.

41. "The Crisis of Contemporary Criticism," *Arion* 6:1, Spring 1967, 38-57. Reprinted, revised, as "Criticism and Crisis," Chapter 1 in BI, 3-19. Reprinted in Morris Philipson and Paul J. Gudel, ed., *Aesthetics Today*, revised edition. New York: New American Library, 1980, 337-51.

42. "Ludwig Binswanger et le problème du moi poétique." In Jean Ricardou, ed., *Les Chemins actuels de la critique* (Colloque de Cerisy, 2-12 September 1966). Paris: Plon, 1967, 77-103; see also de Man's comments at 54, 121-24. Reprinted in 10/18 edition, Paris, 1968, 43-58, no comments. Reprinted in second 10/18 edition, Paris, 1973, 63-89, comments at 49, 106-09. Translated by de Man as "Ludwig Binswanger and the Sublimation of the Self," Chapter 3 in BI, 36-50.

43. "Vérité et méthode dans l'oeuvre de Georges Poulet," *Critique* 266, July 1969, 608-23. Translated by de Man as "The Literary Self As Origin: The Work of Georges Poulet," Chapter 6 in BI, 79-101.

44. "The Rhetoric of Temporality." In Charles S. Singleton, ed., *Interpretation: Theory and Practice*. Baltimore: Johns Hopkins University Press, 1969, 173-209. Reprinted as Chapter 10 in

BI2, 187-228. Part I translated by Peter Grotzer as "Allegorie und Symbol in der Europäischen Fruhromantik." In S. Sonderegger, A. Haas, and H. Burger, ed., *Typologica Litterarum* (Festschrift für Max Wehrli). Zurich: Atlantis, 1969, 403-25. Translated into Italian and Serbo-Croatian in editions of BI.

45. "Literary History and Literary Modernity," *Daedalus* 99:2 [Theory in Humanistic Studies], Spring 1970, 384-404. Reprinted in Morton W. Bloomfield, ed., *In Search of Literary Theory*. Ithaca: Cornell University Press, 1972, 237-67. Reprinted as Chapter 8 in BI, 142-65.

46. "The Riddle of Hölderlin" [review of Friedrich Hölderlin, *Poems and Fragments*], *The New York Review of Books* 15:9, 19 November 1970, 47-52.

47. "Lyric and Modernity." In Reuben A. Brower, ed., *Forms of Lyric*. New York: Columbia University Press, 1970, 151-76. Reprinted as Chapter 9 in BI, 166-86.

48. "The Rhetoric of Blindness: Jacques Derrida's Reading of Rousseau," Chapter 7 in BI, 102-42. Reprinted, substantially revised, as "On Reading Rousseau," *Dialectical Anthropology* 2:1, February 1977, 1-18. First version translated by Jean-Michel Rabaté and Bernard Esmein as "Rhétorique de la cécité" *Poétique* 4, 1970, 455-75.

49. "Foreword," in BI, vii-x.

50. Comments, in Richard Macksey and Eugenio Donato, eds., *The Languages of Criticism and the Sciences of Man* [retitled *The Structuralist Controversy*]. Baltimore: Johns Hopkins University Press, 1970 [1972], 150, 184-85.

51. Review of Jacques Derrida, *De la grammatologie, Annales de la société Jean-Jacques Rousseau* 37, 1966-68 [published 1970], 284-88.

52. "Introduction," Rainer Maria Rilke, *Oeuvres I: Prose*, "édition établie et présentée par Paul de Man," Paris: Editions du Seuil, 1972, 7-8.

53. "Introduction," also "Note sur l'édition," "Note sur les traductions," "Annotation et interprétation," and "Chronologie de la vie de Rainer Maria Rilke," Rainer Maria Rilke, *Oeuvres II: Poésie*, "édition établie et présentée par Paul de Man," Paris: Editions du Seuil, 1972, 7-42, 43-54. Introduction translated by de Man, revised, as "Tropes (Rilke)," Chapter 2 in AR, 20-56.

54. "Proust et l'allégorie de la lecture," in *Mouvements premiers* (Etudes critiques offertes à Georges Poulet), Paris: Librairie José Corti, 1972, 231-50. Translated by de Man, revised, as "Reading (Proust)," Chapter 3 in AR, 57-78.

55. "Literature and Language: A Commentary," *New Literary History* 4:1, Autumn 1972, 181-92. Reprinted as Appendix B in BI2, 277-89.

56. "Genesis and Genealogy in Nietzsche's *Birth of Tragedy*," *Diacritics* 2:4, Winter 1972, 44-53. Reprinted as "Genesis and Genealogy (Nietzsche)," Chapter 4 in AR, 79-102.

57. "Theory of Metaphor in Rousseau's *Second Discourse*," *Studies in Romanticism* 12:2, Spring 1973, 475-98. Reprinted in David Thorburn and Geoffrey Hartman, eds., *Romanticism: Vistas, Instances, Continuities*. Ithaca: Cornell University Press, 1973, 83-114. Also reprinted as "Metaphor (*Second Discourse*)," Chapter 7 in AR, 135-59.

58. "Semiology and Rhetoric," *Diacritics* 3:3, Fall 1973, 27-33. Reprinted, revised, as Chapter 1 in AR, 3-19. Also reprinted in Josué V. Harari, ed., *Textual Strategies: Perspectives in Post-Structuralist Criticism*. Ithaca: Cornell University Press, 1979, 121-40.

59. "Nietzsche's Theory of Rhetoric," *Symposium* 28:1, Spring 1974, 33-51, including question and answer session. Reprinted, without Q & A, as "Rhetoric of Tropes (Nietzsche)," Chapter 5 in AR, 103-18.

60. Review of Harold Bloom, *The Anxiety of Influence: A Theory of Poetry, Comparative Literature* 26:3, Summer 1974, 269-75. Reprinted as "Review of Harold Bloom's *Anxiety of Influence*," Appendix A in BI2, 267-76.

61. "Action and Identity in Nietzsche," *Yale French Studies* 52 [Graphesis: Perspectives in Literature and Philosophy], 1975, 16-30. Reprinted as "Action and Identity in Nietzsche," *Nuova Corrente* 68-69, 1975-6, 570-84. Also reprinted in Robert Young, ed., *Untying the Text: A Post-Struc-

turalist Reader. Boston: Routledge and Kegan Paul, 1981, 266-79. Also reprinted as "Rhetoric of Persuasion (Nietzsche)," Chapter 6 in AR, 119-31. Translated into French by Victoria Bridges and Marie-Hélène Martin-Lambert as "Rhétorique de la persuasion (Nietzsche)," *Po&sie* 33, 1985, 55-65.

62. "The Timid God (A Reading of Rousseau's *Profession de foi du vicaire Savoyard*)," *Georgia Review* 29:3, Fall 1975, 533-58. Reprinted as "Allegory of Reading (*Profession de foi*)," Chapter 10 in AR, 221-45.

63. "Political Allegory in Rousseau," *Critical Inquiry* 2:4, Summer 1976, 649-75. Reprinted as "Promises (*Social Contract*)," Chapter 11 in AR, 246-77.

64. "The Purloined Ribbon," *Glyph* 1, 1977, 28-49. Reprinted as "Excuses (*Confessions*)," Chapter 12 in AR, 278-301.

65. "Foreword," to Carol Jacobs, *The Dissimulating Harmony*. Baltimore: Johns Hopkins University Press, 1978, vii-xiii.

66. "The Epistemology of Metaphor," *Critical Inquiry* 5:1, Autumn 1978, 13-30. Reprinted in Sheldon Sacks, ed., *On Metaphor*. Chicago: University of Chicago Press, 1979, 11-28. Reprinted in Michael Shapiro, ed., *Language and Politics*. New York: New York University Press, 1984, 195-214. Translated into German by Werner Hamacher as "Epistemologie der Metapher." In Anselm Haverkamp, ed., *Theorie der Metapher*. Darmstadt: Wissenschaftliche Buchgesellschaft, 1983, 415-37.

67. "Shelley Disfigured." In Harold Bloom et al., *Deconstruction and Criticism*. New York: Seabury Press, 1979, 39-73. Reprinted as Chapter 6 in RR, 93-123.

68. "Introduction" [to special issue titled "The Rhetoric of Romanticism"], *Studies in Romanticism* 18:4, Winter 1979, 495-99.

69. "Autobiography as De-facement," *MLN* 94:5, December 1979, 919-30. Reprinted as Chapter 4 in RR, 67-81.

70. "Self (*Pygmalion*)," Chapter 8 in AR, 160-87.

71. "Allegory (*Julie*)," Chapter 9 in AR, 188-220.

72. "Preface," in AR, ix-xi.

73. "Pascal's Allegory of Persuasion." In Stephen J. Greenblatt, ed., *Allegory and Representation* (Selected Papers from the English Institute, 1979-80). Baltimore: Johns Hopkins University Press, 1981, 1-25. See also otherwise unpublished remarks of de Man quoted in Greenblatt, "Preface," vii-xiii at viii.

74. "The Resistance to Theory," *Yale French Studies* 63 [The Pedagogical Imperative: Teaching as a Literary Genre], 1982, 3-20. Reprinted as Chapter 1 in RT, 3-20. Translated into Italian by Stefano Rosso as "Sulla resistenza alla teoria," *Nuova Corrente* 93, 1984, 7-34.

75. "Hypogram and Inscription: Michael Riffaterre's Poetics of Reading," *Diacritics* 11:4, Winter 1981, 17-35. Reprinted partially in "Lyrical Voice in Contemporary Theory" [see item 92 below]. Reprinted as Chapter 3 in RT, 27-53.

76. "Introduction," Hans Robert Jauss, *Toward an Aesthetics of Reception*, trans. Timothy Bahti. Minneapolis: University of Minnesota Press, 1982, vii-xxv. Reprinted partially in "Lyrical Voice in Contemporary Theory" [see item 92 below]. Reprinted as "Reading and History," Chapter 4 in RT, 54-72.

77. "A Letter from Paul de Man," *Critical Inquiry* 8:3, Spring 1982, 509-13 [response to Stanley Corngold, "Error in Paul de Man," 489-507].

78. "Sign and Symbol in Hegel's *Aesthetics*," *Critical Inquiry* 8:4, Summer 1982, 761-75.

79. "The Return to Philology" [contribution to "Professing Literature: A Symposium on the Study of English"], *The Times Literary Supplement* 4158, 10 December 1982, 1355-56. Reprinted as Chapter 2 in RT, 21-26.

80. Contribution to "Hommage à Georges Poulet," *MLN* 97:5, December 1982, [vii-viii].

81. "Foreword to Revised, Second Edition," in BI2, xi-xii.

82. "Dialogue and Dialogism," *Poetics Today* 4:1, Spring 1983, 99-107. Reprinted as Chapter 6 in RT, 106-114.

83. "Hegel on the Sublime." In Mark Krupnik, ed., *Displacement: Derrida and After*. Bloomington: Indiana University Press, 1983, 139-53.

84. "Reply to Raymond Geuss," *Critical Inquiry* 10:2, December 1983, 383-90 [response to Geuss, "A Response to Paul de Man," 375-82; cf. "Sign and Symbol in Hegel's *Aesthetics*"].

85. "Phenomenality and Materiality in Kant." In Gary Shapiro and Alan Sica, ed., *Hermeneutics: Questions and Prospects*. Amherst: University of Massachusetts Press, 1984, 121-44.

86. "Wordsworth and the Victorians," Chapter 5 in RR, 83-92.

87. "Anthropomorphism and Trope in the Lyric," Chapter 9 in RR, 239-62. Translated into French by Christian Fournier as "Anthropomorphisme et trope dans la poésie lyrique," *Poétique* 62, April 1985, 131-45.

88. "Aesthetic Formalization: Kleist's *Über das Marionettentheater*," Chapter 10 in RR, 263-90.

89. "Preface," in RR, vii-ix.

90. Stefano Rosso, "An Interview with Paul de Man," *Nuova Corrente* 93, 1984, 303-13. Reprinted as Chapter 7 in RT, 115-21. First published in Italian translation as Maurizio Ferraris and Stefano Rosso, "Da New York: In memoria Paul de Man: L'Ultima intervista," *Alfabeta* 58, March 1984, 12. [Transcript of taped interview with Rosso, conducted 4 March 1983 at Cornell University, broadcast on RAI (Italian National Broadcasting System) radio program, "America Coast to Coast," 1 June 1983.]

91. Robert Moynihan, "Interview with Paul de Man," *The Yale Review* 73:4, Summer 1984, 576-602. [With an introduction by J. Hillis Miller. Taped in 1980.]

92. "Lyrical Voice in Contemporary Theory: Riffaterre and Jauss." In Chaviva Hošek and Patricia Parker, ed., *Lyric Poetry: Beyond New Criticism*. Ithaca: Cornell University Press, 1985, 55-72. [Reprints portions of "Introduction" to Jauss and of "Hypogram and Inscription" with a brief new introduction.]

93. "'Conclusions: Walter Benjamin's 'The Task of the Translator,'" *Yale French Studies* 69 [The Lesson of Paul de Man], 1985, 25-46. Reprinted, including question and answer session following lecture, as Chapter 5 in RT, 73-105.

94. "Jacques Lacan," in French, with an English translation by Shoshana Felman in her "Postal Survival, or the Question of the Navel," *Yale French Studies* 69, 1985, 49-72 at 50-51.

Forthcoming:

(1) *Aesthetic Ideology*, edited by Andrzej Warminski. Minneapolis: University of Minnesota Press, 1987. To include essays on Hegel, Kant, Pascal, "Epistemology of Metaphor," as well as two previously unpublished lectures entitled "Kant's Materialism" (1981) and "Kant and Schiller" (1983).

(2) *Fugitive Essays*, edited by Lindsay Waters. Minneapolis: University of Minnesota Press, 1987. To include previously uncollected essays and reviews.

Note: Paul de Man doubtless wrote and translated more texts than those listed here, especially during the 1940s. A more complete bibliography will thus appear in the future — Tom Keenan.

Index

Index

Paul de Man was Sterling Professor of Humanities at Yale University, where he taught comparative literature. He also taught at Harvard, Cornell, and Johns Hopkins, and held a chair in comparative literature at the University of Zürich. His books include: *Blindness and Insight* (1971, revised edition, Minnesota, 1983), *Allegories of Reading* (1980), and *The Rhetoric of Romanticism* (1984). Two additional posthumous titles are forthcoming from Minnesota: *Aesthetic Ideology* and *Romanticism and Modernism: Essays 1953-70*.

Wlad Godzich teaches comparative literature at the Université de Montréal and at the University of Minnesota, is director of the Center for Humanistic Studies at the University of Minnesota, and is co-editor, with Jochen Schulte-Sasse, of the series Theory and History of Literature.